A Christ-Centered
EASTER

A Christ-Centered
EASTER

DAY-BY-DAY ACTIVITIES TO CELEBRATE EASTER WEEK

EASTER ACTIVITIES FOR LATTER-DAY SAINT FAMILIES

JANET AND JOE HALES

EAGLE GATE
SALT LAKE CITY, UTAH

To our quiver full:

Mallory, Laurel,

Isaac, Christian,

Katherine, Jared,

and Mariah

Visit us at deseretbook.com

Library of Congress Cataloging-in-Publication Data

Hales, Janet.

A Christ-centered Easter : day-by-day activities to celebrate Easter week / Janet and Joe Hales.

p. cm.

Includes bibliographical references.

ISBN 1-57008-779-2 (pbk.)

1. Holy Week—Prayer–books and devotions—English. 2. Easter—Prayer–books and devotions—English. 3. Church of Jesus Christ of Latter-day Saints—Prayer–books and devotions—English. I. Hales, Joe. II. Title.

BV90 .H25 2002
263' .93—dc21 2001007919

Printed in the United States of America 72076-0234R

Publishers Printing, Salt Lake City, UT

10 9 8 7 6 5 4 3

CONTENTS

Acknowledgments

We would like to express our sincere appreciation and gratitude to the following people for their help with this book:

Russell and Ann Orton, for their assistance, advice, and encouragement.

Andrea Richardson, for her ideas and example.

Kris Palmer and Derek Palmer, our visionary muses.

Both of our extended families, for their encouragement and support.

As part of this family effort, particular thanks go to Jane Hales for getting this project rolling; Dow Wilson for reviewing parts of the manuscript and adding gentle but candid editorial advice; Lynne Wilson for her advice born from years of biblical study and research, and for her Palm Sunday story; and Mallory Hales, for her over-the-shoulder wordsmithing.

We also acknowledge Lynne Perry Christofferson, who gave generous permission to use her song, "My Own Little Lamp"; Ida Mae Kempel and Eddie Ogan, for graciously giving permission to use their stories; and Tammy Israelsen, who gave timely advice on craft projects and acted as an ever-present sounding board.

We appreciate all of the help given by the good people at Deseret Book: specifically Jana Erickson for holding our virtual hands; Tom Hewitson for arranging the artwork and design; and Janna DeVore for her gentle persistence and very necessary editorial skills.

Finally, we thank our children, for their encouragement and willingness to "make do" during the Summer of the Manuscript.

Preface

For years I felt that our family's Easter celebration was as hollow as the chocolate bunnies we devoured on Easter morning. All my life I had been told that the atonement and resurrection of Jesus Christ are the most sacred and significant events in all creation. *If that is true*, I reasoned, *then shouldn't Easter—the commemoration of those events—be the highlight of our year?*

It certainly was not the highlight in my family. Christmas, with all those presents *and* candy, was the undisputed favorite in our home, followed by Halloween and then Thanksgiving. Though hard to admit, Easter fell somewhere between Valentine's Day and Independence Day in actual importance to the children.

Quietly, I began to make plans for a new kind of Easter celebration. My modest hope was that I could elevate the celebration of our Lord's resurrection above that of witches and goblins or even of bunnies and eggs.

It didn't take long to review what we normally did for Easter. Although the number and scope of activities seemed to wax and wane from year to year, our main focus rested on eggs and a lot of chocolate. We had few, if any, other traditional activities. There was the special Easter dinner, of course; but with little children underfoot and piles of dishes in the kitchen afterwards, I was so worn out by the end that the meal brought little joy. We had never established the tradition of new clothes for Easter Sunday, and I could never remember any of the Easter bunny songs I had sung in grade school. If we dyed our own eggs and had our Easter egg hunt on Saturday, our festivities lasted, at the most, two days. No wonder we liked Christmas better!

It would be an understatement to say that I believed there was room for improvement. My husband, Joe, had also begun to feel dissatisfied with our family's shallow concept of Easter. With the parents in agreement, then, the stage was set to change our family's Easter focus from Peter Cottontail and his basket to Jesus Christ, his atonement, and his resurrection. We wanted our family to better honor and praise him. We sought to draw nearer to him. And we hoped that this holiday would set a worshipful tone for the entire year.

From year to year our attempts to create a meaningful Easter holiday have gradually grown into a full Holy Week of celebration, filled with inspirational music, stories, activities, and special foods. This book is a compilation of the ideas that we have collected and invented so far.

From Palm Sunday through Easter Sunday, our family enjoys what are now traditional activities corresponding to a simple scripture reading from the Gospels. In years past, our younger children have looked forward to the first day of our celebration, when we act out the Triumphal Entry. Youngest to oldest delight in our Saturday night "Jerusalem Dinner," where we eat a meal like one Jesus might have eaten and in the way he would have eaten it: without utensils and sitting on mats or lying down on cushions. I searched for authentic foods and recipes from biblical times and created a list of foods available to Jesus. Over the years our family has mixed and matched these items into a variety of interesting menus.

For us, as I imagine for everyone who celebrates with young children, this holiday is very much a work in progress. Every year we get new ideas, implement them in the coming celebration, and then vote to retain or discard them in future years. We have had some spectacular failures and some profound successes. There have been meaningful and Spirit-filled discussions about the sacrament and the priesthood and joyful tears as we have read about our resurrected Lord's appearance to Mary Magdalene in the garden. Come Easter morning, our home has been filled with joyful singing and shouts of "He is risen, He is risen!"

As you work to infuse a new spirit into your own Easter celebration, we hope this book will provide helpful and thoughtful activities for your family to copy, embellish, and learn from. Most important, we hope that you will feel the spirit that comes from having a truly Christ-centered Easter.

—JANET HALES

Introduction
How to Use This Book

One word of advice before you throw out the Easter baskets and chocolate bunnies: don't.

When we began our tradition of a weeklong, Christ-centered Easter celebration, we transformed the egg dying, hunt, and candy into a wonderful Spring Celebration held on the first day of spring. When the warm spring days finally break free from winter, we certainly *feel* like celebrating. And now we do! We make Spring Baskets and dye Spring Eggs. Because the first day of spring is always before and independent of Easter, we can cheerfully celebrate springtime with our children. They, in turn, do not feel deprived when we later celebrate the actual Easter holiday in a different way.

Getting Started

In this book, you will find plans for an eight-day Easter week celebration that lasts from Palm Sunday to Easter Sunday. The foundation for this celebration rests on the biblical accounts of Jesus Christ's last week in mortality. Our family substitutes these passages of scripture for our normal family scripture study that week. Additionally, we usually complete one or more daily activities associated with the biblical events discussed that day. Throughout Easter week, we sing songs, read stories, and eat special foods. Every year we redesign our holiday to be as relaxed or as structured, as modest or as grand, as best fits the family's preferences and needs.

Our most successful celebrations begin with a family meeting held a week before Palm Sunday. We usually devote an entire family home evening to organizing and planning our Easter week.

What follows is an outline of our Easter week plans. In planning your week of activities and devotionals, remember that you do not need to do everything. Your daily devotional can be as simple as you'd like. Modify it to best fit your needs. It is useful to first establish a visual framework for the entire eight days by making an outline that stretches across eight sheets of paper, one sheet for each day. Record the pertinent information, needs, and assignments for each of the eight days on the appropriate pages and tape the sheets together. Post the entire outline in a central location in your home to act as a guide for your celebration.

To begin planning, schedule a time each day for your family scripture study and daily devotional or activity. Using this book as a reference, decide which activities your family will use to celebrate each day of the week. This planning session is the ideal time to choose any Easter hymns you will learn and sing, the special foods you will eat (indicating what you will need to purchase and make beforehand), and any acts of service your family will perform. This advanced scheduling will do much to ensure the successful implementation of your plans and prevent your Easter week from becoming either overscheduled or haphazard.

After the organizational meeting is over, develop separate to-do lists for each day of Easter week. Use the recipes and activity instructions in this book to create a comprehensive shopping list of everything needed during the week. Transfer pertinent details of the to-do lists to your large family outline. The

Saturday before Palm Sunday is usually a convenient day for one big shopping trip to buy recipe ingredients and other needed items.

How This Book Is Organized

This book is divided into two parts. Part 1 includes eight sections—one for each day of the Holy Week—that will help you prepare meaningful discussions and give you ideas for establishing a Christ-centered Easter celebration in your home. The chapters are numbered according to the day and provide an overview for the day's celebration. Each day includes the text of selected biblical prophecies that foretell or refer to the events of that day in Christ's life; scripture reading references; points of family discussion; and a list of ideas from which to select a meaningful story, project, role-play, or other activity to complete that day's celebration.

The letters to the left of each suggested activity represent the approximate age group for which the activity is designed. While a loose grouping such as this is bound to have many exceptions, it will nonetheless provide a basis from which to choose activities that are age-appropriate for your family. The letters and their corresponding age groups are as follows:

- P Preschoolers (ages 3 to 5)
- G Grade schoolers (ages 6 to 12)
- T Teenagers (ages 13 to 17)
- A Adults
- F Entire family

Part 2 includes seven sections of material that provide additional information about activities, food preparation, and other details for each day described in Part 1. Following is an outline of these supplementary chapters and a brief explanation of their contents:

Sacred Music and Hymns

Singing songs about the Savior during Easter week brings a wonderful spirit of love and reverence into our home. Each year we sing songs learned in Primary as well as hymns learned from past Holy Week celebrations. We typically choose two new hymns to learn during our daily devotionals: a hymn about the Atonement, to sing specifically during our Passover meal, and a hymn about the Resurrection, to sing throughout Easter day.

This section includes a list of suggested songs that we have found appropriate to learn for our Easter week celebration. It also includes a list of sacred and classical music that can be played throughout the week to uplift and edify your family.

Stories with a Message

Stories are a great teaching tool and can often captivate three-year-olds and thirteen-year-olds all at the same time. The lists of suggested activities for each day in Part 1 include story ideas. In some cases, we simply give you the reference for the story and trust that you'll be able to find the story in the *Ensign* or *Friend*. At times, however, we have suggested using a story that is less accessible. This section includes the text of these stories.

The Jewish Sabbath

This section is a short presentation on the importance of the Jewish Sabbath, and briefly describes how the apostles might have felt the Sabbath after Christ's crucifixion.

Easter Activities and Plays

This section includes details for carrying out the activities and performing the role-plays suggested for each day in Part 1 of this book.

A Passover Celebration and Jerusalem Dinner

As our family slowly converted from Easter egg hunts and candy to a Christ-centered Easter celebration, we recognized the need to retain some festivity and, of course, some good food.

Our efforts in this area are detailed in this section.

Each year, we reserve Thursday night for a discussion and activity centered on the Passover, followed by a special meal with our children. This festive meal has become meaningful and significant, especially as we have reserved a short time before the meal to explain the Passover and help our children more clearly understand the backdrop against which our Lord's sacrifice began.

If your children are too young to understand and appreciate the symbolism behind the Passover, you may want to have the Jerusalem Dinner on Thursday night instead. Or, have the Jerusalem Dinner on Saturday night and enjoy two nights of special dinners.

This section will give you all the details you need to prepare the ritual foods for Passover. It includes recipes and explanations about the foods and symbolism involved.

It also includes details for the Jerusalem Dinner activity and the recipes needed to prepare the foods suggested for other days of the week.

A Parallel Account of the Gospels

Scriptural references from the accounts of Matthew, Mark, Luke, and John specific to each day of Jesus' last week are provided in Part 1 of this book and can be used for your daily family scripture study.

Each of the four Gospels writers contributes unique and diverse detail to the story of the Savior's last week. In our daily review of these references, we have tried to present our children with a cohesive narrative of the week. At first, we awkwardly flipped back and forth between various authors to present the information in chronological order and point out any differences in the narratives. Eventually we found a remedy for all of this page turning: we cut and pasted an electronic copy of the King James Version of the Bible and assembled the four gospel accounts side by side in parallel columns on the same page. This allows for much more freedom and ease of use during our scripture reading. It is now almost effortless to weave a single composite story with detail from each of the four Gospel accounts or, if we choose, to compare each account and select the day's reading from the author who provides the most detail for the point we wish to make. This section of the book includes a copy of our parallel account.

To prepare our account, we relied primarily upon the Harmony of the Gospels chronology found in the Bible Dictionary of the LDS edition of the King James Version of the Bible. This Bible Dictionary chronology is attributed to Elder Bruce R. McConkie, who is understood to be the principal editor of the dictionary. At various points we also consulted *Jesus the Christ* by James E. Talmage (for the order of events at the Last Supper) and *Our Lord of the Gospels* by J. Reuben Clark, Jr. (for the order of events at the Crucifixion).

In some cases, the suggested sequence of events led to a change in the order of verses. When verses have been moved from their original numerical order within a specific Gospel, the verse numbers have been set in boldface type. Most scriptural accounts of the Gospels make no record of events that may have occurred on Wednesday. Therefore, the readings for Day 3 and Day 4 are shown in our account in one section. Feel free to divide the reading between Tuesday and Wednesday.

You can find additional versions of parallel Gospel accounts at the library or your local bookstore. Two good references are:

Thomas M. Mumford, *Horizontal Harmony of the Four Gospels in Parallel Columns* (Salt Lake City: Deseret Book, 1976).

Steven J. Hite and Julie M. Hite, comp., *The New*

Testament with the Joseph Smith Translation: Includes All Textual Changes Made by the Prophet Joseph Smith and the Four Gospels in Chronological Harmony and Parallel Columns (Orem, Utah: Veritas Group, 1994).

Useful Reference Materials for Children, Youth, and Adults

Though a parallel account of the Gospels is very helpful, our younger children have still understood little of our Bible reading. This has necessitated that we, as parents, be able to explain the words, customs, and history of New Testament times. And this has, of course, required some extra study on our part. *The New Testament for Latter-day Saint Families* (Bookcraft, 1998), the Bible Dictionary, and *Jesus the Christ* (James E. Talmage [Classics in Mormon Literature Edition], Salt Lake City: Deseret Book, 1982) have been particularly helpful in this endeavor.

This section lists further bibliographic information for books, magazine articles, videos, audiotapes, and music that will aid you in answering questions and enhancing your own understanding of specific topics. The following abbreviations are used throughout the text when noting these two common references:

BD—the Bible Dictionary found in the Church-published King James Version of the Bible

JTC—*Jesus the Christ*

This section also includes detailed maps of the Holy Land and city of Jerusalem to provide a visual framework of the last week of the Savior's life.

A Final Note

Although we now celebrate for the entire week, Easter is definitely my favorite day. After honoring the Savior with seven days of devotionals, activities, and quiet reflection, the presence of the Holy Spirit in our home and hearts on this day is overwhelmingly joyous and humbling. As Joe and I bear witness of Jesus Christ to our children on Easter day, we try to capture and mirror the feelings and emotions of those who were eyewitnesses to Jesus' resurrection. The children's Spirit-filled responses to our attempts have been the greatest benefit of our efforts to celebrate a more Christ-centered Easter.

As busy parents of seven small children, taking time to write this activity book was not in our initial plans. But in the course of trying to enhance our family's understanding and appreciation of Jesus Christ, that is what happened. We hope that you will find the ideas in this book useful, and that you will take the liberty to expand and modify them to best assist your own family in honoring our Savior and making your Easter holiday a celebration of the Savior, his atonement, and his resurrection.

Part 1
Easter Week, Day by Day

Day 1—Palm Sunday

Jesus' Triumphal Entry

Prophecy: *"Rejoice greatly, O daughter of Zion; shout, O daughter of Jerusalem: behold, thy King cometh unto thee: he is just, and having salvation; lowly, and riding upon an ass, and upon a colt the foal of an ass"* (Zechariah 9:9).

Scripture Reading: Matthew 21:1–11; Mark 11:1–11; Luke 19:28–44; John 12:12–36

Ideas for Family Discussion:

- Discuss the symbolism of using palm branches to usher the Lord into Jerusalem (see Dorothy D. Warner, "Exploring: Palms for the Lord," *Friend*, March 1996, 26–27, for a good reference).
- Discuss the meaning of the word *Hosanna* and why we shout it, even today, at temple dedications and on other solemn occasions (see BD, "Hosanna," 704–5; *JTC*, chapter 29, note 8).
- Discuss what your family would do to show your joy that Jesus is the Christ if he came today.

Suggested Activities:

F Choose both a Resurrection Hymn and an Atonement Hymn to learn during the week. (Use *Hymns of The Church of Jesus Christ of Latter-day Saints*, Salt Lake City: The Church of Jesus Christ of Latter-Day Saints, 1985; see also page 14 of this book.)

F Make a story line of pictures to display on your wall, mantel, or bookshelf as a visual reminder of the Easter story. Each day add a new picture that corresponds with the events of that day; or display the entire Easter story in pictures at once. Try using pictures from the Gospel Art Kit (GAK), available from the Church Distribution Center. You could also use various issues of the *Ensign* (January 1991 is a particularly good issue).

F Begin your Easter week with a "LOA" (Love One Another) table or wall. Cover a table or wall with poster board or butcher paper. Encourage everyone to write complimentary notes to each other on the poster board throughout the week. Keep a pen and a jar of candy near the table to encourage participation. Read the comments aloud on Easter Sunday.

F Encourage family members to use their daily prayers to ask, "Whom can I serve today?" Report personal service experiences on Easter Sunday.

F Read "A Miracle on Palm Sunday" (pages 18–19 of this book).

G P Make faux palm branches out of cardboard (for spines) and green paper.

G P Act out the "Triumphal Entry Play" (page 26 of this book).

G P Go on a nature walk with your children. Instruct them to find a variety of objects that are significant to the Easter story. For example, have them find a branch to signify the palm branches thrust at Jesus' feet as he rode a donkey into Jerusalem; a thorn to represent the crown of thorns Jesus wore on his head; a piece of wood to signify the cross to which Jesus was nailed; a rock to represent the stone rolled away from the open tomb; and so on.

Day 2—Monday

Cleansing the Temple

Prophecy: *"Even them will I bring to my holy mountain, and make them joyful in my house of prayer: their burnt offerings and their sacrifices shall be accepted upon mine altar; for mine house shall be called an house of prayer for all people"* (Isaiah 56:7).

Scripture Reading: Matthew 21:12–18; Mark 11:12–19; Luke 19:45–48

Ideas for Family Discussion:

- Discuss the progression of the temple cleansing as it applies to our own lives: purging, learning, receiving blessings (healing), praising (see Matthew 21:12–16).
- Discuss, on a personal level, the healings that took place in the temple. How might you have felt if you had been there?
- Given Jesus' action in the temple, discuss how he would feel in your own family's home? How might he cleanse it? As a family, choose one way to purify your home and make that your goal for the week.

Suggested Activities:

F Read "The Rich Family in Our Church" (pages 19–21 of this book) and plan a family service/sacrifice to perform in celebration of Jesus' atonement.

F Complete "The Easter Story in Eggs" activity (pages 26–28 of this book).

F Name, list, and discuss some of Jesus' character traits (obedient, forgiving, kind, compassionate, humble, patient, selfless, courageous, filial, and so on). Choose one to work on as a family during the week.

F Have "secret pals" this week. Write out the names of each family member on separate slips of paper and put them into a hat. Have each person draw a name. Encourage family members to treat their "secret pals" as Jesus would treat them if he were here. Report successes on Easter Sunday.

G P Use pictures to tell the Easter story (GAK, pictures 118, 223–34). Ask questions such as: Why were the people so happy when Jesus came back to Jerusalem? How do you think his friends felt when Jesus was crucified? What did the woman think when she saw that Jesus' body wasn't in the tomb? Why did Jesus tell people to touch his resurrected body? How do you think his friends felt after they realized that Jesus still lived?

G P Read "The First Easter" by Julie Wardell (*Friend*, April 1988, 20–21).

G P Discuss and practice pronouncing words such as *Messiah*, *Atonement*, *Crucifixion*, and *Resurrection*.

P Put Easter story cutout figures (cutout set 8, #33248, Church Distribution), in a hat. Have children draw out a figure(s) and place it in chronological order on a flannel board as a parent tells the Easter story.

P Make up hand motions for Easter Primary songs while singing them.

Day 3—Tuesday

Parables and Teachings

Prophecy: *"I will open my mouth in a parable: I will utter dark sayings of old"* (Psalm 78:2).

Scripture Reading: (Spread these readings over the next two days) Matthew 21:19–26:16; Mark 11:20–14:11; Luke 20:1–22:6; John 12:37–50

Specific Parables and Teachings:

- Question of Authority: Matthew 21:23–27
- Parable of the Two Sons: Matthew 21:28–32
- Parable of the Wicked Husbandman: Matthew 21:33–46
- Parable of the Royal Marriage Feast: Matthew 22:1–14
- Tribute to Caesar: Matthew 22:15–22
- The Great Commandment: Matthew 22:34–46
- Condemnation of Hypocrisy and Lament over Jerusalem: Matthew 23
- The Widow's Mite: Mark 12:41–44
- Parable of the Ten Virgins: Matthew 25:1–13
- Parable of the Entrusted Talents: Matthew 25:14–30
- Parable of the Final Judgment: Matthew 25:31–46

Ideas for Family Discussion:

- Discuss the definition of the word *parable* and why Jesus used parables as a teaching method (see BD, "Parables," 740–41; *JTC*, chapter 19, "'He Spake Many Things unto Them in Parables'").
- Choose a parable or teaching as the focus of an in-depth discussion (see *JTC*, chapters 30–32; Robert Millet, *Parables and Other Teaching Stories* [Salt Lake City: Deseret Book, 1999], various sections). Use questions such as the following to begin your discussion:

  Regarding the Widow's Mite, Why were people throwing money into the treasury? What is a mite? What does the widow's money represent? How are all sincere followers of Christ like the poor widow?

  Regarding the Parable of the Royal Marriage Feast, What does the marriage symbolize? Who is the bride? Who do the various invited parties represent? What does the wedding garment symbolize and why is it so important? What application does this have in our lives?

Suggested Activities:

F Read Stephen E. Robinson's "Parable of the Bicycle" (in "Believing Christ," *Ensign*, May 1992, 5–9, specifically 8–9).

F Act out a parable. Wear costumes, use props, and record it on videotape so the children can view it later.

F Make Oil Lamps to use when discussing the Parable of the Ten Virgins (page 28 of this book).

T G Play parable charades.

A T G Make up your own parable with modern and/or ancient meaning.

DAY 4—WEDNESDAY

REST IN BETHANY

Note: No events are specifically recorded for this day. It is assumed that Jesus spent the day in Bethany. You may continue to use parables taught on Day 3 or discuss later verses, such as Mary anointing the Savior and Judas bargaining for the betrayal of Christ (both are scriptural accounts found at the end of the reading text for Day 3).

Prophecy: *"And I said unto them, If ye think good, give me my price; and if not, forbear. So they weighed for my price thirty pieces of silver"* (ZECHARIAH 11:12).

Ideas for Family Discussion:

- Define the words *anoint* and *spikenard.* Explain possible reasons why the woman anointed Jesus (SEE BD, "ANOINT," 609; *JTC*, CHAPTER 29, NOTE 7).
- Explain that thirty pieces of silver was the price commonly paid for the life of a male slave. Use the following questions to discuss Judas' betrayal: Why did the Pharisees set this price? Would it have mattered to Judas how much money had been offered? Has Jesus ever been betrayed since then? What has been the price?

Suggested Activities:

F While reading and discussing the Parable of the Ten Virgins, burn two lamps: one filled with oil and another containing only a very little oil. Turn off all other lights and burn both lamps until the foolish virgin's lamp burns out.

F Sing and discuss "My Own Little Lamp" (pages 16–17 of this book).

G P Act out the play "The Parable of the Ten Virgins" (page 29 of this book).

DAY 5—THURSDAY

THE LAST SUPPER AND JESUS' PRAYER AND AGONY IN GETHSEMANE

Prophecies: *"Yea, my own familiar friend, in whom I trusted, which did eat of my bread, hath lifted up his heel against me"* (PSALM 41:9).

"Reproach hath broken my heart; and I am full of heaviness: and I looked for some to take pity, but there was none; and for comforters, but I found none" (PSALM 69:20).

"Surely he hath borne our griefs, and carried our sorrows: yet we did esteem him stricken, smitten of God, and afflicted" (ISAIAH 53:4).

Scripture Reading: MATTHEW 26:17–75; MARK 14:12–72; LUKE 22:7–65; JOHN 13:1–18:27

Ideas for Family Discussion:

- Read Matthew 26:17–19 and discuss what you might do to prepare for Passover. Have the family participate in the Jewish tradition of cleaning the house in preparation for the Passover.
- Read John 13:4–15 and discuss why it was important that Jesus wash the apostles' feet (SEE *JTC*, CHAPTER 33, "THE ORDINANCE OF THE WASHING OF FEET"; NOTE 3).
- Discuss the significance of the sacrament and having the authority of the Melchizedek Priesthood on the earth today.

- Read and discuss Christ's description of his own suffering in Doctrine and Covenants 19:16–19.
- Discuss how it would feel to be part of the mob arresting Jesus and then have him heal you (SEE LUKE 22:50–51).
- Discuss the illegalities of Jesus' Jewish trial (SEE *JTC*, CHAPTER 34, NOTE 4).
- Discuss what Peter might have felt before and after the cock crowed (SEE MATTHEW 26:69–75).

Suggested Activities:

[F] Read "The Belayer" (pages 21–22 of this book).

[F] Sing an Atonement hymn.

[A] [T] Eat the ritual foods of Passover and a special dinner prepared with foods common in Jesus' day (pages 35–39 of this book).

[A] [T] [G] Encourage family members to ask in personal prayer, "What can I do to be more worthy to partake of the sacrament this Sunday?" Challenge them to make a concerted effort to follow the inspiration they receive.

DAY 6—FRIDAY

JESUS' TRIAL AND CRUCIFIXION

Prophecies: *"He was oppressed, and he was afflicted, yet he opened not his mouth: he is brought as a lamb to the slaughter, and as a sheep before her shearers is dumb, so he openeth not his mouth"* (ISAIAH 53:7).

"I gave my back to the smiters, and my cheeks to them that plucked off my hair: I hid not my face from shame and spitting" (ISAIAH 50:6).

"For dogs have compassed me: the assembly of the wicked have inclosed me: they pierced my hands and my feet" (PSALM 22:16).

"My God, my God, why hast thou forsaken me? why art thou so far from helping me, and from the words of my roaring?" (PSALM 22:1).

"He keepeth all his bones: not one of them is broken" (PSALM 34:20).

Scripture Reading: MATTHEW 27:1–61; MARK 15:1–47; LUKE 22:66–23:56; JOHN 18:28–19:42

Ideas for Family Discussion:

- Discuss, in more depth, various aspects of Christ's suffering by asking the following questions: Did Jesus fully understand what he was required to do? What did Jesus mean when he said, "Nevertheless, not as I will, but as thou wilt?" What is the equivalent of that submission in our own lives?
- Discuss whether Pilate was able to divest himself of responsibility by washing his hands (SEE MATTHEW 27:24).
- Discuss Jesus' responsibility for and care of his mother (SEE JOHN 19:26–27).
- Compare and contrast events after the Crucifixion as experienced in the Old World versus the New World (SEE LUKE 23:44–47; 3 NEPHI 8:5–23).

Suggested Activities:

[G] [F] Do the "Easter Story Cookies" activity (pages 30–31 of this book).

[A] [T] [G] Craft a crown of thorns using thorny branches found in your area (branches from a honey locust tree, rose bush, and so on).

Be sure to wear sturdy gloves when making the crown.

A T G Obtain a heavy wooden beam and try to carry it.

T G P Taste the difference between water and vinegar.

F Turn out all the lights for the evening to signify the three hours of darkness in the Old World and the three days in the New World (SEE MATTHEW 27:45; 3 NEPHI 8:20–23).

F Sing the Crucifixion hymn chosen on Day 1.

DAY 7—SATURDAY

THE JEWISH SABBATH

Prophecy: *"Verily, verily, I say unto you, That ye shall weep and lament, but the world shall rejoice: and ye shall be sorrowful, but your sorrow shall be turned into joy"* (JOHN 16:20).

Scripture Reading: MATTHEW 27:62–66; LUKE 23:56

Ideas for Family Discussion:

- Using the text on pages 24–25 of this book, discuss Jewish Sabbath observance.
- Read 1 Peter 3:18–20 and Doctrine and Covenants 138:29–37. Discuss the mercy of vicarious work as part of the plan of redemption. Discuss the irony that Christ's death brought grief to his disciples on earth but joy to those in the spirit world. Ask your family, What might this teach us about trusting in the Lord with patience?

Suggested Activities:

T G Do the "Plan of Happiness Treasure Hunt" (pages 31–34 of this book).

F Eat a Jerusalem Dinner, like one Jesus may have eaten in Jerusalem (pages 39–43 of this book).

A G Prepare the dough for Easter Breakfast Rolls to serve Easter morning (pages 42–43 of this book).

DAY 8—EASTER SUNDAY

JESUS' RESURRECTION AND APPEARANCES

Prophecy: *"He will swallow up death in victory; and the Lord God will wipe away tears from off all faces; and the rebuke of his people shall he take away from off all the earth: for the Lord hath spoken it"* (ISAIAH 25:8).

Scripture Reading: MATTHEW 28:1–15; MARK 16:1–12; LUKE 24:1–49; JOHN 20:1–23

Ideas for Family Discussion:

- Discuss the range of emotions that must have been felt by Mary Magdalene or Mary the mother of Jesus on this day (from continued shock and despair to hope and unbounded joy).
- Discuss how the apostles reacted to Mary

Magdalene's report that Christ had risen (Mark 16:10–11) and the report of the two men on the road to Emmaus (Mark 16:13). Discuss the Lord's response to this (Mark 16:14).

- Discuss how we can correctly discern the truth ourselves. (Though not exclusive, specific spiritual discernment through revelation is given by right to worthy supplicants through the gift of the Holy Ghost. The light of Christ gives general spiritual discernment to everyone [Moroni 7:16].)
- Thomas was not with the other ten apostles at the resurrected Lord's appearance in Jerusalem and would not subsequently believe what they had seen. Eight days later, however, Christ appeared again, and this time Thomas was in the company. Discuss how Christ's words to Thomas, both gentle and reproving, can help us in our efforts to live by faith (John 20:24–29).

Suggested Activities:

[F] Awaken the children with Handel's "Hallelujah Chorus" from the *Messiah*.

[F] Meet in the morning for an Easter devotional: Sing the Resurrection Hymn your family chose on Day 1. Offer a prayer of praise and thanksgiving. Retell the sacred story of the resurrected Lord's first appearances as found in John and Luke (John 20:1–18; Luke 24:13–35). Share personal testimonies of Christ's atonement and resurrection.

[F] Start a new tradition: prepare a special Easter breakfast to eat during your morning devotional.

[F] Read "What Was in Jeremy's Egg?" (pages 22–23 of this book).

[F] Eat an Easter dinner of broiled fish and honeycomb (page 43 of this book) while reading about Jesus' visitation to his apostles in Luke 24:36–53.

[F] Invite a guest to have Easter dinner with the family.

[F] If you made a "LOA" table earlier in the week, read all of the comments aloud.

[A] [T] [G] If you chose to participate in such an activity, report on service given throughout the week, both as a result of prayerful asking and as given to "secret pals."

[A] [T] Read several Psalms, such as 23, 24, 100, 113, 136, 146, and 149, and then write a family psalm of praise.

[A] [T] Encourage family members to spend some scheduled time in personal reflection. Suggest that they devote an entire prayer to thanksgiving; write down their testimonies of Jesus as the Christ; study and ponder the sacrament prayers (D&C 20:77, 79); or take a personal inventory of their lives by praying, reflecting, and recommitting.

Part 2
Supplementary Material and Activity Helps

Sacred Music and Hymns

Music for Everyone to Sing

The following songs come from Hymns of The Church of Jesus Christ of Latter-day Saints, *Salt Lake City: The Church of Jesus Christ of Latter-day Saints, 1985.*

Atonement and Crucifixion Hymns

"Behold the Great Redeemer Die," no. 191
"God Loved Us, So He Sent His Son," no. 187
"How Great the Wisdom and the Love," no. 195
"I Stand All Amazed," no. 193
"There Is a Green Hill Far Away," no. 194
"Upon the Cross of Calvary," no. 184

Resurrection Hymns

"Christ the Lord Is Risen Today," no. 200
"He Is Risen!" no. 199
"I Believe in Christ," no. 134
"I Know That My Redeemer Lives," no. 136
"Jesus, Once of Humble Birth," no. 196
"My Redeemer Lives," no. 135

The following songs come from Children's Songbook, *Salt Lake City: The Church of Jesus Christ of Latter-day Saints, 1989.*

Children's Hymns

"Beautiful Savior," 62
"Did Jesus Really Live Again?" 64
"He Died That We Might Live Again," 65
"He Sent His Son," 34
"Hosanna," 66
"I Feel My Savior's Love," 74
"Jesus Has Risen," 70
"Jesus Said Love Everyone," 61
"Love One Another," 136
"Tell Me the Stories of Jesus," 57
"The Sacrament," 72

Background Music

The following list includes specific songs and albums that we have listened to during Easter week. Many of the songs can be found on a variety of recordings. Those listed are merely suggestions. Other recordings of the same pieces can be found at your local library or music store.

Bach, Johann Sebastian. "The Easter Oratorio." *Bach: Easter Oratorio, Magnificat.* Ton Koopman, Amsterdam Baroque Orchestra. Wea/Atlantic/Erato audio CD 23416.

Bach, Johann Sebastian. "St. Matthew's Passion." *Bach—Matthäus-Passion.* Kiri Te Kawana, Ann Sofie von Otter, Sir Georg Solti, et al. Uni/London classics audio CD 25691.

Baroque Duet. Kathleen Battle, Wynton Marsalis. Sony Classics audio CD 46672.

Brahms, Johannes. "Ein Deutsches Requiem" (A German Requiem). *Brahms—Ein Deutsches Requiem.* Robert Shaw, dir., Atlanta Symphony Orchestra. Telarc audio CD 80092.

Children's Songbook. Disc 2. The Church of Jesus Christ of Latter-day Saints. Audio CD 623336 (Church Distribution #50505).

Dowdle, Michael. *Fifty Favorite Hymns.* Joyspring Records audio CD.

Dowdle, Michael. *Hymns of Praise, Songs of Joy.* Joyspring Records audio CD.

Handel, George Frideric. *Handel—Messiah*. Sir Colin Davis, dir., London Symphony Orchestra and Chorus. Uni/Philips audio CD 38356.

Hymns of The Church of Jesus Christ of Latter-day Saints. Music only. The Church of Jesus Christ of Latter-day Saints (CHURCH DISTRIBUTION #50866).

Mormon Tabernacle Choir. *Make a Joyful Noise*. Jerold D. Ottley, dir. Sony Classics audio CD 61984.

Mormon Tabernacle Choir. *O Divine Redeemer*. The Church of Jesus Christ of Latter-day Saints (CHURCH DISTRIBUTION #80845).

Rachmaninoff, Sergei. *Vespers*. Robert Shaw, dir. Telarc audio CD 80172.

Rutter, John. "Requiem." *Requiem & Magnificat*. Collegium audio CD 504.

My Own Little Lamp

Words & Music by
LYNNE PERRY CHRISTOFFERSON

lis - ten for His gen - tle voice and then I will know that these things are right and my
own lit - tle lamp will be filled with light.
1.
2.
filled with light, and my own lit - tle lamp will be filled with
light.

Stories with a Message

A Miracle on Palm Sunday

by Lynne Wilson

My eight-year old son, Abe, had been ill for the better part of four months by the time we flew from our home in Belgium back to the United States to have him admitted to Children's Hospital in Milwaukee. It was just before Palm Sunday 1998.

His illness started before Christmas, when he and his sister, Mariah, came down with severe headaches—so severe that they could not move, could not bear to have the lights on, and could not even bend their necks. It seemed like a classic case of meningitis to me, but the neighborhood doctor came to our home and ruled that out. So for two weeks, the two of them just lay still in their beds. The headaches slowly began to subside. At least Mariah's did.

Abe got better at first, but had a recurrence of the same symptoms in early January. This cycle continued almost every two weeks for the next four months. We kept him as flat as possible during these relapses to minimize his dizziness. I carried him from room to room to use the bathroom, to study his science videos for home schooling, and to join the family for scripture study in the evenings. During his relapses, he ate most of his meals through a straw while lying down. As a result, he lost much weight. With each return of ill health, he seemed to be worse than ever before. By early March he was so lethargic and emaciated that he could barely speak.

The doctors were unable to determine what was wrong. After many prayers and blessings, Abe had bounced back so thoroughly each time that we would rejoice in his seemingly complete recovery. One of these rebounds occurred the Sunday before his baptism. He and I were home from church watching general conference videos and studying his baptism preparation book. In the book, we read a quote from Moroni 7:26.

"And after that he came men also were saved by faith in his name; and by faith, they become the sons of God. And as surely as Christ liveth he spake these words unto our fathers, saying: Whatsoever thing ye shall ask the Father in my name, which is good, in faith believing that ye shall receive, behold, it shall be done unto you."

Abe and I both felt impressed that through our faith in Jesus Christ he could be healed. I knelt by his bedside and poured out our need for the Lord's help. Abe poured out his faith. He was filled with the spirit of healing, and within thirty minutes was up and walking again. He was well enough to be baptized the following Sunday. It was a Pentecostal feeling.

The headaches recurred, however. One week after his baptism he was again bedridden. We felt prompted to take him to the States for another medical perspective.

By the end of March, Abe was a patient at Children's Hospital in Milwaukee. The MRI showed a large cyst, the size of an egg, at the base of his skull. The emotional trauma of the hospital setting, with so many doctors and jet lag thrown in, made Abe as sick as he had ever been. Nevertheless, on Palm Sunday I received permission to take him from the hospital and carry him to church for sacrament meeting.

I took Abe to our former ward in Milwaukee. I bore my testimony and pleaded for the prayers and faith of the congregation on behalf of my boy. Our former bishop agreed to give him a blessing just after the service. Abe was laid on the bishop's desk while three or four close friends circled the table and laid their hands on his head to give him a priesthood blessing. Abe was promised that he would not yet die but would live to hold the priesthood and go to the temple. We were filled with hope and focus. By the time we returned to the hospital, Abe was determined to do his part in getting better.

Abe became a living example of faith in practice. With all the faith an eight-year-old can muster, he said, "If I am going to be able to pass the sacrament, then I will have to learn to sit up again." So he struggled for what seemed to be a very long time, until he could finally sit up. The room kept spinning and his head throbbed, but he was determined to have those promises fulfilled. We spent the next hour slowly helping him walk to the bathroon back. "If I am going to pass the sacrament, then I will have to learn how to walk again!"

By the time the dinner trays came by, Abe had an appetite and was sitting up to eat. By the time the doctor came by for his evening visit, Abe greeted him by walking down the hallway. Dr. K. was astounded and exclaimed, "How appropriate for a miracle to have occurred on Palm Sunday! I hope you don't mind that I asked the ten o'clock mass to pray for our Abe."

This gracious gift of healing was a mini-restoration of Abe's body. That Easter week we became keenly aware and grateful for the eternal gift of our Savior's atonement, his life and suffering, his love and resurrection. We understood more fully that Jesus did not suffer only for our sins, but for our weaknesses, our illnesses, our pain, and our sorrows. We felt that we had just experienced, on a personal level, a little of Christ's passion—his suffering, his death, and rebirth—in Abe's life. A ram had been found in the thicket for our Abraham.

(Previously unpublished. Used with Permission.)

The Rich Family in Our Church

By Eddie Ogan

I'll never forget Easter 1946. I was fourteen, my little sister Ocy was twelve, and my older sister Darlene was sixteen. We lived at home with our mother, and the four of us knew what it was to do without many things. My dad had died five years before, leaving Mom with seven schoolkids to raise and no money. By 1946 my older sisters were married and my brothers had left home. A month before Easter the pastor of our church announced that a special Easter offering would be taken to help a poor family. He asked everyone to save and give sacrificially.

When we got home, we talked about what we could do. We decided to buy fifty pounds of potatoes and live on them for a month. This would allow us to save twenty dollars of our grocery money for the offering. Then we thought that if we kept our electric lights turned out as much as possible and didn't listen to the radio, we'd save money on that month's electric bill. Darlene got as many house and yard cleaning jobs as possible, and both of us baby-sat for everyone we could. For fifteen cents we could buy enough cotton loops to make three potholders to sell for one dollar each. We made twenty dollars on potholders. That month was one of the best of our lives.

Every day we counted the money to see how much we had saved. At night we'd sit in the dark and talk about how the poor family was going to enjoy having the money the church would give them. We had about eighty people in church so we figured that whatever amount of money we had to give, would surely be multiplied twenty times after everyone had contributed. After all, the pastor had reminded us to save for the sacrificial offering every Sunday for a month.

The day before Easter, Ocy and I walked to the grocery store and got the manager to give us three crisp twenty-dollar bills and one ten-dollar bill for all our change. We ran all the way home to show Mom and Darlene. We had never had so much money before. That night we were so excited we could hardly sleep. We didn't care that we wouldn't have new clothes for Easter; we had seventy dollars for the sacrificial offering. We could hardly wait to get to church!

On Sunday morning, rain was pouring. We didn't own an umbrella, and the church was over a mile from our home, but it didn't seem to matter how wet we got. Darlene had cardboard in her shoes to fill the holes. The cardboard came apart, and her feet got wet. We sat in church proudly. I heard some teenagers talking about the Smith girls having on their old dresses. I looked at the teenagers who spoke and glanced at their new clothes, and I felt rich.

When the sacrificial offering was taken, we were sitting on the second row from the front. Mom put in the ten-dollar bill, and each of us kids put in a twenty. As we walked home after church, we sang all the way. At lunch Mom had a surprise for us. She had bought a dozen eggs, and we had boiled Easter eggs with our fried potatoes!

Late that afternoon the minister drove up in his car. Mom went to the door, talked with him for a moment, and then came back with an envelope in her hand. We asked what it was, but she didn't say a word. She opened the envelope and out fell a bunch of money. There were three crisp twenty-dollar bills, one ten, and seventeen one-dollar bills. Mom put the money back in the envelope. We didn't talk; we just sat and stared at the floor.

We had gone from feeling like millionaires to feeling like poor white trash. We kids had such a happy life that we felt sorry for anyone who didn't have our Mom and Dad for parents and a house full of brothers and sisters and other kids visiting constantly. We thought it was fun to share silverware and see whether we got the spoon or the fork that night. We had two knives that we passed around to whoever needed them. I knew we didn't have a lot of things that other people had, but I had never thought we were poor. That Easter day I found out we were.

The minister had brought us the money for the poor family, so we must be poor. I didn't like being poor. I looked at my dress and worn-out shoes and felt so ashamed—I didn't even want to go back to church. Everyone probably knew we were poor!

I thought about school. I was in the ninth grade and at the top of my class of more than one hundred students. I wondered if the kids at school knew that we were poor. I decided that I could quit school since I had finished the eighth grade. That was all the law required at the time. We sat in silence for a long time. Then it got dark and we went to bed. All that week, we girls went to school and came home, and no one talked much.

Finally on Saturday, Mom asked us what we wanted to do with the money. What did poor people do with money? We didn't know. We didn't want to go to church on Sunday, but Mom said we had to. Although it was a sunny day, we didn't talk on the way. Mom started to sing, but no one joined in, and she only sang one verse.

At church we had a missionary speaker. He talked about how many people in the country he served lacked even the necessities of life, and how much the missionary work could benefit from donations made by the congregation. He ended with a plea, asking us "to help these poor people." We looked at each other and smiled for the first time in a week.

Mom reached into her purse and pulled out the envelope. She passed it to Darlene. Darlene gave it to me, and I handed it to Ocy. Ocy put it in the offering.

When the offering was counted, the minister announced that it was a little more than one hundred dollars. The missionary was excited. He hadn't expected such a large offering from our small church. He said, "You must have some rich people in this church."

Suddenly it struck us! We had given eighty-seven of that "little more than one hundred dollars." We were the rich family in the church! Hadn't the missionary said so? From that day on I've never been poor again. I've always remembered how rich I am because I have Jesus!

The Belayer

BY JANET HALES

One winter our family reunioned with relatives in Indiana. The Midwest was unseasonably cold that year so we mostly stayed indoors. After a few days captive in a house with thirteen children and nine adults, it was a relief to get out and make a day of visiting the Indianapolis Children's Museum.

We had a wonderful time! One of the most popular exhibits in the museum was the climbing wall. Most of the children were eager to try it, although it was so high that it almost reached the rafters. I was surprised that even our seven-year-old son, who was notoriously afraid of heights, wanted to climb. We gave our permission, and he excitedly began to buckle himself into the climbing gear.

Each climber, along with a designated helper, had to undergo brief training before attempting the climb. As a rule, my motivation to keep my son from killing himself is quite high, so I volunteered and listened intently to the instructions. Each helper was called a "belayer" and provided a fail-safe system for the climbers. The belayer braces himself below the wall and holds onto a rope that snakes around an overhead beam before attaching to the harness of the climber. If the climber should slip, the belayer can stop the climber's fall by holding tightly onto the lifeline in his hands. Though our coach admitted that many children slip off the face of the wall while climbing, I was reassured that as long as I didn't let go of the rope my son would only swing through the air until he could again get a toehold on the wall.

Responsibility for my son's safety weighed on me, and I felt tense and nervous during his entire climb. He was the youngest climber on the wall and struggled as he slowly scaled to the top. More than halfway up his foot slipped and he began to fall. I saw him misstep and reflexively pulled on the rope swinging him up into the air. He thought it was great fun—I thought it was about time for him to get a new belayer.

I remembered my feelings as a belayer some months later when reading about a terrifying climbing experience of Alan Czenkusch, the head of a rock climbing school. Czenkusch was scaling up a high precipice while his belayer was braced on a ledge below him. Suddenly, Czenkusch slipped and tumbled backward in free fall. The force of his fall on the rope ripped three climbing braces out of the rock and jerked his belayer off the ledge. Plunging through space, the death of both men seemed certain had it not been for the belayer's unbelievable strength and presence of mind. With outstretched arms, he reached for the rock face, found a hold, and clung to it—arresting his own fall and jerking Czenkusch to a halt just ten feet above the ground.

"'Don saved my life,' the climber later commented. 'How do you respond to a guy like that? Give him a used climbing rope for a Christmas present? No. You remember him. You *always* remember him'" (IN ERIC ANDERSEN, "THE VERTICAL WILDERNESS," *PRIVATE PRACTICE*, NOVEMBER 1979, 21).

My mind jumped back from our adventure at the Children's Museum to an upper room in ancient Jerusalem. I recognized again that Jesus Christ arrested our free fall to death more surely and completely than any mortal man has ever saved another. Perfect in his love, in his life, and in his sacrifice, he first broke bread as a reminder and then asked that we remember him—that we *always* remember him.

WHAT WAS IN JEREMY'S EGG?

BY IDA MAE KEMPEL

Jeremy was born with a twisted body and slow mind. At the age of 12 he was still in second grade, seemingly unable to learn. His teacher, Doris Miller, often became exasperated with him. He would squirm in his seat, drool and make grunting noises.

At other times, he spoke clearly and distinctly, as if a spot of light had penetrated the darkness of his brain. Most of the time, however, Jeremy irritated his teacher. One day, she called his parents to come to St. Theresa's for a consultation. As the Forresters sat quietly in the empty classroom, Doris said to them, "Jeremy really belongs in a special school. It isn't fair to him to be with younger children who don't have learning problems. Why, there is a five-year gap between his age and that of the other students!"

Mrs. Forrester cried softly into a tissue, while her husband spoke. "Miss Miller," he said, "there is no school of that kind nearby. It would be a terrible shock for Jeremy if we had to take him out of this school. We know he really likes it here."

Doris sat for a long time after they left, staring at the snow outside the window. Its coldness seemed to seep into her soul. She wanted to sympathize with the Forresters. After all, their only child had a terminal illness. But it wasn't fair to keep him in her class. She had 18 other youngsters to teach, and Jeremy was a distraction. Furthermore, he would never learn to read and write. Why waste any more time trying?

As she pondered the situation, guilt washed over her. "Oh God," she said aloud, "here I am complaining when my problems are nothing compared to that poor family! Please help me to be more patient with Jeremy!"

From that day on, she tried hard to ignore Jeremy's noises and his blank stares. Then one day, he limped to her desk, dragging his bad leg behind him. "I love you, Miss Miller," he exclaimed, loud enough for the whole class to hear. The other students snickered, and Doris' face turned red. She stammered, "Wh-why that's very nice, Jeremy. N-now please take your seat."

Spring came, and the children talked excitedly about the coming of Easter. Doris told them the story of Jesus, and then to emphasize the idea of new life springing forth, she gave each of the children a large plastic egg. "Now," she said to them, "I want you to take this home and bring it back tomorrow with something inside that shows new life. Do you understand?"

"Yes, Miss Miller!" the children responded enthusiastically—all except for Jeremy. He just listened intently; his eyes never left her face. He did not even make his usual noises.

Had he understood what she had said about Jesus' death and resurrection? Did he understand the assignment? Perhaps she should call his parents and explain the project to them. That evening, Doris' kitchen sink stopped up. She called the landlord and waited an hour for him to come by and unclog it. After that, she still had to shop for groceries, iron a blouse and prepare a vocabulary test for the next day. She completely forgot about phoning Jeremy's parents.

The next morning, 19 children came to school, laughing and talking as they placed their eggs in the large wicker basket on Miss Miller's desk. After they completed their math lesson, it was time to open the eggs.

In the first egg, Doris found a flower. "Oh yes, a flower is certainly a sign of new life," she said. "When plants peek through the ground we know that spring is here." A small girl in the first row waved her arm. "That's my egg, Miss Miller," she called out.

The next egg contained a plastic butterfly, which looked very real. Doris held it up. "We all know that a caterpillar changes and grows into a beautiful butterfly. Yes, that is new life, too." Little Judy smiled proudly and said, "Miss Miller, that one is mine!"

Next, Doris found a rock with moss on it. She explained that moss, too, showed life. Billy spoke up from the back of the classroom, "My daddy helped me!" he beamed.

Then Doris opened the fourth egg. She gasped. The egg was empty! Surely it must be Jeremy's, she thought, and of course, he did not understand her instructions. If only she had not forgotten to phone his parents! Because she did not want to embarrass him, she quietly set the egg aside and reached for another.

Suddenly Jeremy spoke up. "Miss Miller, aren't you going to talk about my egg?" Flustered, Doris replied, "But Jeremy—your egg is empty!" He looked into her eyes and said softly, "Yes, but Jesus' tomb was empty, too!"

Time stopped. When she could speak again, Doris asked him, "Do you know why the tomb was empty?" "Oh yes!" Jeremy said, "Jesus was killed and put in there. Then His Father raised Him up!"

The recess bell rang. While the children excitedly ran out to the school yard, Doris cried. The cold inside her melted completely away.

Three months later, Jeremy died. Those who paid their respects at the mortuary were surprised to see 19 eggs on top of his casket, all of them empty.

THE JEWISH SABBATH

Much has been made in the Christian world of the many restrictions that Jewish religious leaders of Jesus' day imposed on Sabbath activity (SEE *JTC*, CHAPTER 15, NOTE 1). Jesus taught that "the sabbath was made for man, and not man for the sabbath: Therefore the Son of man is Lord also of the sabbath" (MARK 2:27–28). When Christ faulted the Jews with reference to the fourth commandment, it was because of their overzealous—and misguided—attempts to keep the Sabbath sacred. Their overemphasis on man-made rules had caused them to disregard the Lord of the Sabbath.

But our understanding of the Jewish Sabbath should not rely solely on scriptural references that record Jesus' rejection of the rigid Jewish Sabbath observance; we must understand the spiritual meaning that underlies many of the rules and regulations.

The Lord declared that the injunction to keep the seventh day holy originated during the creation of the world (SEE EXODUS 20:11). For six days, the Lord created the world and everything in it. Jewish tradition says that on the seventh day, he completed his work by creating peace and rest. He called the first six days "good," reserving the Sabbath day to call holy.

To the Jew who observes an orthodox Sabbath, it is an anticipated day of joy and celebration, of laughter and song, of rest from the profane, and of worship of the sacred. Jewish law and tradition specifically prohibit sadness on this day. Talk of war and politics, problems and pain, are for the other days of the week. On the seventh day, Jews commemorate and celebrate their relationship with God. To many in the world, it may seem ironic that those of the Jewish faith believe strict rules and prohibitions will bring them true freedom. For Latter-day Saints, however, this concept is not foreign. We too seek to restrict the outside world from encroaching upon the day sanctified by God, to subdue the headlong rush of the everyday grind and make possible the embrace of the sublime.

Jews who observe the commandment to keep the Sabbath day holy imitate their Creator, albeit on a small scale, as they create a fitting Sabbath each week. Restrictions against lighting fires, working one's trade, walking too far, and, nowadays, using the telephone or television, effectively reduce one's life to its most basic and important elements: God and family. Creating such a weekly sanctuary takes deliberate and premeditated effort. This effort, however, is rewarded by restoring a proper perspective to the other six days of the week.

Orthodox Sabbath observance in modern times follows traditions that are millennia old. Family members prepare for the Sabbath by taking ritual baths and dressing in their best clothing. Friday evening, with everything prepared and in place, Jewish mothers perform the significant ritual of "kindling the Holy lights." In Christ's day, a Hebrew woman would have lit lamps. Today she lights candles. She covers her head, lights the candles, and prays—specifically signaling a transition from the secular to the sacred.

Strangers and the less fortunate are often asked to share the family's Sabbath dinner, and the table is beautifully set for that evening with a special tablecloth and the family's best dishes. Part of that dinner always includes two loaves of bread twisted together as one. The loaves are an important symbol of God's Sabbath, and their significance hearkens back to the time of Moses and the children of Israel, who wandered in the wilderness for forty years. Every Friday morning, in preparation for the Sabbath day, the Lord sent the Israelites double their normal portion of manna. Every week, the Lord not only blessed his people with Sabbath sustenance but provided for their rest as well. To this day, the Orthodox Jew remembers and emulates.

Saturday is a day of family worship and celebration, of disciplined reverence balanced by joy. Joy in being sons and daughters of God. Joy in freedom through the Lord. Joy in his approbation and his tutelage. As Truman Madsen aptly wrote about the Jewish Sabbath, "To miss the joy is to miss it all" (*The Radiant Life* [Salt Lake City: Bookcraft, 1994], 73; see also pp. 70–85 for a particularly good discussion on the Jewish Sabbath).

It was against this Sabbath-day backdrop that the disciples of our Lord grappled with the reality and cruelty of Jesus' death. Perhaps the shock of it all shielded them from the searing irony of their grief on this Sabbath day—a day of supposed gladness. Only one day away from exquisite joy borne of understanding, the sorrow and confusion of Jesus' followers on this Sabbath must have seemed overpowering and infinite. A reading of the scriptural accounts leads us to assume that each disciple felt abandoned to a dark night of hopelessness—with little dreaming of the brilliant Light prepared to dawn the next day.

EASTER ACTIVITIES AND PLAYS

TRIUMPHAL ENTRY PLAY

Suggested Cast

Narrator
Disciple(s) sent in search
Christ
Donkey colt
Donkey's owner(s)
Disciples shouting "Hosanna"

Narrative of Events

1. Disciples are sent in search of donkey (MARK 11:1–3).
2. Disciples find donkey and owners (MARK 11:4).
3. Owners question disciples' intentions (MARK 11:5–6).
4. Clothing is draped on colt; Jesus sits upon it and rides into Jerusalem (MARK 11:7).
5. Many disciples cut down palm branches and shout "Hosanna" while waving the branches and spreading them and clothing in the path of the donkey (MARK 11:8–10).

THE EASTER STORY IN EGGS

Preparatory Work

1. Obtain twelve plastic eggs and number them with a permanent marker from one to twelve. (Put the eggs in an empty egg carton for easy storage.)
2. Photocopy and cut out the scripture passages that follow.
3. Gather the indicated visual aids.
4. Place each scripture strip and its corresponding visual aid into the numbered eggs.

Instructions

Your family can do this activity in several ways:

- "Serve" the eggs with dinner at each place setting and open the eggs in sequential order during the meal.
- Play "scrambled eggs." Throw the scriptures, visual aids, and eggs in a bag. As each is drawn out, separately match the visual aids with the scriptures in sequence, or match the scriptures with the visual aids and eggs. End the activity by reading each scripture in order.
- Take turns opening each egg in sequence and reading the enclosed scripture.

Scriptures

1. "Then one of the twelve, called Judas Iscariot, went unto the chief priests, and said unto them, What will ye give me, and I will deliver him unto you? And they covenanted with him for thirty pieces of silver. And from that time he sought opportunity to betray him" (MATTHEW 26:14–16).

2. "And as they were eating, Jesus took bread, and blessed it, and brake it, and gave it to the disciples, and said, Take, eat; this is my body. And he took the cup, and gave thanks, and gave it to them, saying, Drink ye all of it; For this is my blood of the new testament, which is shed for many for the remission of sins" (MATTHEW 26:26–28).

3. "Then cometh Jesus with them unto a place called Gethsemane, and saith unto the disciples, Sit ye here, while I go and pray yonder. And he took with him Peter and the two sons of Zebedee, and began to be sorrowful and very heavy. . . . And he went a little further, and fell on his face, and prayed, saying, O my Father, if it be possible, let this cup pass from me: nevertheless not as I will, but as thou wilt. . . . He went away again the second time, and prayed, saying, O my Father, if this cup may not pass away from me, except I drink it, thy will be done. . . . And he left them, and went away again, and prayed the third time, saying the same words" (MATTHEW 26:36–37, 39, 42, 44).

4. "When the morning was come, all the chief priests and elders of the people took counsel against Jesus to put him to death: And when they had bound him, they led him away, and delivered him to Pontius Pilate the governor" (MATTHEW 27:1–2).

5. "Pilate saith unto them, What shall I do then with Jesus which is called Christ? They all say unto him, Let him be crucified. And the governor said, Why, what evil hath he done? But they cried out the more, saying, Let him be crucified. When Pilate saw that he could prevail nothing, but that rather a tumult was made, he took water, and washed his hands before the multitude, saying, I am innocent of the blood of this just person: see ye to it" (MATTHEW 27:22–24).

6. "And the soldiers led him away into the hall, called Praetorium; and they call together the whole band. And they clothed him with purple, and platted a crown of thorns, and put it about his head, and began to salute him, Hail, King of the Jews! And they smote him on the head with a reed, and did spit upon him, and bowing their knees worshipped him" (MARK 15:16–19).

7. "And as they led him away, they laid hold upon one Simon, a Cyrenian, coming out of the country, and on him they laid the cross, that he might bear it after Jesus. And there followed him a great company of people, and of women, which also bewailed and lamented him. . . . And when they were come to the place, which is called Calvary, there they crucified him, and the malefactors, one on the right hand, and the other on the left" (LUKE 23:26–27, 33).

8. "Then said Jesus, Father, forgive them; for they know not what they do. And they parted his raiment, and cast lots" (LUKE 23:34).

9. "Jesus, when he had cried again with a loud voice, yielded up the ghost. And, behold, the veil of the temple was rent in twain from the top to the bottom; and the earth did quake, and the rocks rent. . . . Now when the centurion, and they that were with him, watching Jesus, saw the earthquake, and those things that were done, they feared greatly, saying, Truly this was the Son of God" (MATTHEW 27:50–51, 54).

10. "And, behold, there was a man named Joseph, a counsellor; and he was a good man, and a just: (The same had not consented to the counsel and deed of them;) he was of Arimathaea, a city of the Jews: who also himself waited for the kingdom of God. This man went unto Pilate, and begged the body of

Jesus. And he took it down, and wrapped it in linen, and laid it in a sepulchre that was hewn in stone, wherein never man before was laid." "And laid it in his own new tomb, which he had hewn out in the rock: and he rolled a great stone to the door of the sepulchre, and departed" (LUKE 23:50–53; MATTHEW 27:60).

11. "And when the sabbath was past, Mary Magdalene, and Mary the mother of James, and Salome, had bought sweet spices, that they might come and anoint him. And very early in the morning the first day of the week, they came unto the sepulchre at the rising of the sun. And they said among themselves, Who shall roll us away the stone from the door of the sepulchre?" (MARK 16:1–4).

12. "And entering into the sepulchre, they saw a young man sitting on the right side, clothed in a long white garment; and they were affrighted. And he saith unto them, Be not affrighted: Ye seek Jesus of Nazareth, which was crucified: he is risen; he is not here: behold the place where they laid him" (MARK 16:5–6).

Visual Aids

1. Three dimes
2. A small cracker or piece of bread
3. A sacrament cup
4. A length of twine
5. A piece of soap
6. A swatch of purple cloth
7. A nail
8. Two toothpicks (to represent casting lots)
9. A bag of crushed rocks and potting soil
10. Strips of white cloth
11. Spices tied in a small piece of cloth
12. Leave this egg empty

OIL LAMPS

Instructions: Clay Lamps

1. Mold pottery clay or Sculpy® into a shallow, watertight bowl with a solid, flat bottom. You can coil a thin "snake" of clay around itself several times to form the bowl shape; or you can use your fingers to flatten and pinch a ball of clay into the bowl shape.

2. Pinch together a small section of the bowl's upper lip to form a small spout, like that on a teapot, just wider than the wick you plan to use. This is the wick channel.

3. Dry the bowl in the sun or according to package instructions.

4. After the lamp has thoroughly dried, wedge a string of candlewick into the wick channel so that about one inch of the wick sticks out above the bowl and the rest of it is coiled in the bottom of the bowl. (If using Sculpy®, line the spout opening with a generous amount of tin foil before wedging the wick in place. This will prevent the clay from melting.)

5. Fill the bowl with oil and wait for the oil to soak up the length of the wick.

6. Light the wick.

Instructions: Lamp Wicking

Wicks can be made in a variety of ways. We have had the best success using a ¼–½-inch strip of cotton (we cut up a terrycloth rag) or woolen cloth as the wick. Twisted cotton, wool fibers, and lengths of 100 percent jute twine make fine wicks. You can even make an adequate wick out of a twisted napkin. Candle wicking can also be purchased from craft stores.

The Parable of the Ten Virgins Play

Cast

Narrator
Wise virgins (up to five)
Foolish virgins (up to five)
Bridegroom
Members of the wedding party with the Bridegroom
Midnight crier
Oil Merchant(s)

Props

Lamps (homemade lamps, fancy jars, or paper cut-outs)
Extra oil containers (cruets, bottles, jugs)
Scarves, jewelry, etc. to be worn by the virgins
Robe and hat to be worn by the bridegroom
A "turban" and robe for the oil merchants
A door to be closed upon the foolish virgins

Narrative of Events

1. The ten virgins wait with lighted lamps outside the bridegroom's house for his arrival. Of the virgins, half are designated "wise" and carry an extra supply of oil with them. Half are "foolish" and have chosen to bring only their lamps (SEE MATTHEW 25:1–4).
2. The bridegroom is later than expected and the virgins fall asleep while waiting for him (SEE MATTHEW 25:5).
3. At midnight, a cry is heard, announcing the bridegroom's arrival (SEE MATTHEW 25:6).
4. Each virgin awakens and trims her lamp (adjusts the wick and oil level to maximize the lamplight) (SEE MATTHEW 25:7).
5. The foolish virgins vainly attempt to borrow extra oil from the wise virgins because their lamps have run out of oil (SEE MATTHEW 25:8).
6. The wise virgins direct the foolish virgins to run and buy more oil from the oil merchants (SEE MATTHEW 25:9).
7. While the foolish virgins are gone buying more oil, the bridegroom comes with the rest of the wedding party. He opens the door of his house, and the wise virgins enter his house with him. The bridegroom closes the door after them (SEE MATTHEW 25:10).
8. The foolish virgins come back and ask to be let into the house. The bridegroom denies them admittance (SEE MATTHEW 25:11–12).

Easter Story Cookies

Ingredients and Props

1 cup whole pecans
1 teaspoon vinegar
3 egg whites
Pinch of salt
1 cup sugar
1 zipper baggie
1 wooden spoon
Masking tape
Bible

Directions and Activity

1. Preheat oven to 300° F.

2. Place pecans in a zipper baggie and let children beat them with a wooden spoon to break them into small pieces.

   Explain that after Jesus' arrest, he was beaten by Roman soldiers. Read John 19:1–3, *"Then Pilate therefore took Jesus, and scourged him. And the soldiers platted a crown of thorns, and put it on his head, and they put on him a purple robe, and said, Hail, King of the Jews! and they smote him with their hands."*

3. Let each child smell the vinegar. Pour 1 teaspoon vinegar into the mixing bowl.

   Explain that when Jesus was thirsty on the cross he was given vinegar to drink. Read John 19:28–30, *"After this, Jesus knowing that all things were now accomplished, that the scripture might be fulfilled, saith, I thirst. Now there was set a vessel full of vinegar: and they filled a spunge with vinegar, and put it upon hyssop, and put it to his mouth. When Jesus therefore had received the vinegar, he said, It is finished: and he bowed his head, and gave up the ghost."*

4. Add egg whites to vinegar.

   Tell the children that eggs represent life.

   Explain that Jesus gave his life so that we could be resurrected and have eternal life. Read John 10:10–11, *"The thief cometh not, but for to steal, and to kill, and to destroy: I am come that they might have life, and that they might have it more abundantly. I am the good shepherd: the good shepherd giveth his life for the sheep."*

5. Sprinkle a little salt into each child's hand. Let them taste it and brush the rest into the bowl.

   Explain that this represents the salty tears shed by Jesus' followers during the crucifixion. Read Luke 23:27, *"And there followed him a great company of people, and of women, which also bewailed and lamented him."*

   Ask your children if any of the ingredients used to this point seem very appetizing.

6. Add 1 cup sugar.

   Explain that the sweetest part of the Easter story is that Jesus died because he loves us. He wants us to know and belong to him and be able to return to the Father. Read Psalm 34:8, *"O taste and see that the Lord is good: blessed is the man that trusteth in him."* Read John 3:16, *"For God so loved the world, that he gave his only begotten Son, the whosoever believeth in him should not perish, but have everlasting life."*

7. Beat with a mixer on high speed for 12 to 15 minutes, until stiff peaks are formed.

   Explain that the color white represents the purity, in God's eyes, of those whose sins have been cleansed by Jesus. Read Isaiah

1:18, *"Come now, and let us reason together, saith the Lord: though your sins be as scarlet, they shall be as white as snow; though they be red like crimson, they shall be as wool."*

8. Fold in the broken nuts. Drop the dough by teaspoons onto a cookie sheet covered with wax paper.

   Explain that each mound of dough represents the rocky tomb where Jesus' body was laid. Read Matthew 27:57–60, *"When the even was come, there came a rich man of Arimathaea, named Joseph, who also himself was Jesus' disciple: He went to Pilate, and begged the body of Jesus. Then Pilate commanded the body to be delivered. And when Joseph had taken the body, he wrapped it in a clean linen cloth, and laid it in his own new tomb, which he had hewn out in the rock: and he rolled a great stone to the door of the sepulchre, and departed."*

9. Put the cookie sheet into the oven, close the door and turn the oven OFF. Give each child a piece of tape and help them seal the oven door.

   Explain that Jesus' tomb was sealed. Read Matthew 27:65–66, *"Pilate said unto them, Ye have a watch: go your way, make it as sure as ye can. So they went, and made the sepulchre sure, sealing the stone, and setting a watch."*

10. Go to bed! Or proceed with the events of the night and leave the cookies in the oven until morning.

    Explain that the children might feel sad to leave the cookies in the oven overnight. Jesus' followers despaired when the tomb was sealed. Read John 16:20, 22, *"Verily, Verily, I say unto you, That ye shall weep and lament, but the world shall rejoice: and ye shall be sorrowful, but your sorrow shall be turned into joy. . . . And ye now therefore have sorrow: but I will see you again, and your heart shall rejoice, and your joy no man taketh from you."*

11. Before the children are up the next morning, remove the tape and open the oven door. After the children awaken, gather them in the kitchen and give everyone a cookie. Tell them to notice how the surface is cracked and to take a bite. The cookies will be hollow.

    Explain that on the first Easter Jesus' followers were amazed to find the tomb open and empty. When they understood what it meant, they rejoiced! Read John 11:25–26, *"I am the resurrection, and the life: he that believeth in me, though he were dead, yet shall he live: And whosoever liveth and believeth in me shall never die."*

Plan of Happiness Treasure Hunt

Preparatory Work and Instructions

1. Prepare a set of messages and a set of clues to be used in a treasure hunt through the house or out in the yard, or both. Write the messages and clues, in numerical order, on individual slips of paper. (Sample messages and clues follow these instructions.)
2. Prepare the "treasure"—a fancy dessert or something else your children really enjoy.
3. Hide all of the clues throughout the house.
4. Hide the treasure in the spot determined by the last clue of the hunt.
5. Before the hunt, let your children know

what the treasure is. Explain that this treasure represents eternal life.

6. Designate Dad or an older son to play the part of the disembodied Christ after his crucifixion. Give him all of the prepared messages.

7. Draw a child's name from a hat and designate that child as a spirit in spirit prison. Explain that this child will pretend to be a person who died without a testimony of the truth and now resides in spirit prison. Briefly review the plan of salvation and tell the children that after Jesus' resurrection, spirits in spirit prison could receive the message of the gospel and choose whether to accept or reject the gospel plan. Explain that this child's primary role is to find the treasure, but that he or she may not interact with or directly receive any clues from the person playing the role of Jesus. The rest of the family will play righteous (and helpful) spirits in paradise. These spirits can travel throughout the house and interact with both the person playing Jesus and the child playing the spirit in spirit prison. (All of our righteous spirits prefer to follow the spirit around as he hunts for the treasure.)

8. Give the child the Introductory Message (see below) and send him or her into a bedroom (spirit prison) to wait until otherwise instructed (this will occur when he or she receives the first message and clue).

9. Have the person playing Jesus organize the "righteous spirits" by giving each child at least one message to deliver to the repentant spirit in "spirit prison" at the proper time. You may want to read all of the messages and clues out loud at this time so that each of the "righteous spirits" knows what the others are doing.

10. The "righteous spirit" with the first message will begin the treasure hunt by delivering it to the child in "spirit prison." Each "righteous spirit," in turn, will deliver his message at the proper time

11. After finding the treasure, allow the entire family to enjoy it while discussing Doctrine and Covenants 138.

Sample Messages and Clues

- Introductory Message (to be given to the child before going into "spirit prison"): *You have just heard something about the good news of a Redeemer and his gospel. You want to learn more. Read this letter:*

  Dear One,

  I love you! I have always loved you. I am thrilled that you want to learn more about following Father and enjoying the blessings he has promised to give each of his children if they are faithful. Please have faith that this promised treasure is better than anything you have ever dreamed possible. As your Redeemer, I cannot come to you personally, but have organized, and will soon send, missionary messengers to teach you about my gospel. My sacrifice, along with your sincere repentance and good works, will enable you to progress as much as you wish to and obtain all that you desire. I hope this means that you will choose to live with Father and me forever in joy and peace.

  Your Savior and Friend,
  Jesus

- Message 1: *You have had the gospel explained to you. You realize that you have sinned and that there is a better way. You desire to change how you think and act. Use the following clue to find clue number 2.*

Behind.
Big and shiny.
Black ebony and white ivory.
Bought with inheritance money.
Beautiful melodies.

[Clue 2 will be hidden behind the piano. Once the child reaches the piano, another righteous spirit will hand him message 2 to read before looking at the second clue. The treasure hunt will proceed in like manner until the treasure has been found.]

- Message 2: *You have accepted Jesus as your personal Savior and have sincerely repented, calling upon him to wash away your sins through his atoning sacrifice.*
- Clue 2:

England's Encyclopedia.
Under "Easter."
Index

[Clue 3 will be tucked in the Encyclopedia Britannica's index, under the word *Easter.* Remember to have a "righteous spirit" give the child message 3 to read before following the directions in clue 3.]

- Message 3: *Wonderful news! Your-great-great grandchild on earth has just been baptized for you in a temple of the Lord. You have accepted the ordinance and are now washed clean.*
- Clue 3:

Four wheels in a line.
Laces up the boot.
Thrown together in a spot.
With lots of other loot.

[Clue 4 will be hidden inside an inline skate in a box of sports equipment. Remember to have a "righteous spirit" give the child message 4 to read before following the directions in clue 4.]

- Message 4: *You are continuing to perfect your ability to love and serve while waiting for the next ordinance to be performed for you on earth.*
- Clue 4:

Wrapping presents?
You will need some shears, tape,
and, of course, paper.
Tie it up, a bow on top,
a loving birthday caper!

[Clue 5 will be inside the box of gift-wrapping supplies. Remember to have a "righteous spirit" give the child message 5 to read before following the directions in clue 5.]

- Message 5: *Great rejoicing! A temple patron is performing the ordinance of the temple endowment in your name. You accept it with great joy.*
- Clue 5:

Some eat lunch
from bags that are brown
Or use them for groceries
when shopping downtown.
At our house,
things are quite different from that—
Brown bags full of wheat,
50 pounds in a stack.

[Clue 6 will be tucked between two stacked bags of wheat in the food storage section of the basement. Remember to have a "righteous spirit" give the child message 6 to read before following the directions in clue 6.]

- Message 6: *You are full of happiness and hope, almost prepared to enjoy the treasure Father has promised to those who follow his Son. You continue to serve others while waiting for the last of the temple work to be done for you.*
- Clue 6:

"These are way too tight!"
My little piggies' are screamin'.

I tell my Mommy nicely
about my piggies' meanin'.
"Go down to the store!" says she,
a smilin' and a grinnin'.
She knows that store's *no store at all,*
just hand-me-downs she's keepin'.

[Clue 7 will be taped on the shoe-storage shelves in the basement. Remember to have a "righteous spirit" give the child message 7 to read before following the directions in clue 7.]

- Message 7: *Wonderful news! Righteous servants on earth have just performed the temple sealing work for you, your spouse, and your children. Now you can be a forever family!*
- Clue 7:

While swinging and slipping
down the slide,
the summer's sun is beating—
I'd better step inside.

The house is cool and shady,
but I'm still burning red.
I'll go to where the ice cubes live,
and stick in my whole head!

[A half gallon of the children's favorite frozen custard will be in the freezer with the words *eternal life* taped to the side. The message below is taped on top of the lid.]

- Treasure Message: *Congratulations! You have found the treasure you desire! Enjoy it with those who have helped you along the way. Run and get spoons, bowls, and your Doctrine and Covenants. Dad wants to discuss section 138 with us while we enjoy!*

A Passover Celebration and Jerusalem Dinner

What You Will Need to Prepare the Ritual Passover Foods

- *Zeroa*, a roasted shankbone of lamb
- *Beitzah*, a roasted egg
- *Maror*, the bitter herbs (romaine lettuce or horseradish)
- *Haroset*, a mixture of apples, nuts, cinnamon, and wine (or grape juice)
- *Karpas*, parsley or another green herb, such as watercress or lettuce
- Three squares of *Matzah* (unleavened bread)
- Food for a meal similar to one that would have been eaten in Jesus' day (recipes begin on page 38).

The Passover

Many Christians, including Latter-day Saints, have drawn upon Jewish tradition by celebrating Passover with an annual meal or celebration to commemorate the symbolism of the holy event. Indeed, Passover is a very sacred occasion. So sacred, in fact, that some Jews feel it is sacrilege to invite non-Jews to participate. Keep this in mind as you plan your own celebration. And take time to reflect on the holy—though festive—nature of Passover. The inclusion of a Passover meal in your family's Easter week is meant to be respectful of things that are not only enlightening to us but also important and sacred to others.

Historical Origins

Jews have celebrated Passover since the time of Moses. Instructed and empowered by the Lord, Moses used both miracles and plagues in an attempt to soften Pharaoh's heart and encourage him to release the Israelites from slavery. Pharaoh remained unmoved. At last, the Lord declared that the Egyptians' final punishment would result in the death of every firstborn child and beast in the land. At the same time, the Israelites were given specific instructions to follow so the destruction would "pass over" their households: Those Israelites who sacrificed and ate a specially selected lamb and marked their doorposts with its blood would be spared the death of their firstborn. Exactly as foretold, the Egyptians suffered loss in every household, while the Israelites who obeyed were spared. Horrified by the destruction, Pharaoh entreated the Israelites to leave quickly, which they did—ending hundreds of years of slavery in Egypt. In commemoration of their redemption from slavery, the Feast of Unleavened Bread—or Passover—has been celebrated annually thereafter, with only a few periods of interruption.

In our day, a ceremonial Passover dinner begins the seven-day Feast of Unleavened Bread. Conservative and Orthodox Jews living outside of Israel celebrate this feast for eight days, with the formal meal being held on the first two nights of Passover.

We choose to celebrate Easter week with a special meal because the New Testament teaches us that the Last Supper was, in fact, a Passover meal. Learning about the symbolism of the ritual Passover foods teaches us about the Savior and the meaning his life and actions have had on people of all religions.

The Ritual Foods

Recipes for the ritual foods eaten in a ceremonial Passover meal begin on page 38. It is not clear when all of these foods were adopted into the ceremony. The wine, the bitter herb, and unleavened bread date to the original ceremony, of course. Others, as specific symbols of Passover, may have pre-dated Jesus Christ, while some were clearly added after the destruction of the temple in Jerusalem in A.D. 70. In the many rabbinical commentaries on the Passover, each ritual food has been interpreted in various ways. For the meal described in this book, we have chosen the explanations that best point toward the Messiah as our Redeemer.

For your Passover activity, we suggest that you prepare each of these ritual foods in small amounts. Take some time before eating to explain to your children what the foods symbolize. Then allow each person to taste the bitter herb, *Haroset*, parsley, and *Matzah*. Afterward, enjoy a meal made up of foods eaten in Jesus' day and discuss the important and sacred events of the Passover celebration that included the Last Supper.

Zeroa. On the eve of their sudden release from Egyptian bondage, Israelite heads of household were to personally select and then sacrifice unblemished lambs in front of congregated Israel. We now know that this was done in similitude of Jesus Christ's sacrifice. The Savior, who is also called the Lamb of God, was perfect in both spirit and body. He voluntarily, and publicly, sacrificed his life for all people and thereby vicariously redeemed us from the bondage of death and sin.

To ensure that the destroying angel of God would "pass over" their homes, the Israelites were told not only to properly select, sacrifice, and eat the Passover (Paschal) lamb, but also to collect its blood and paint it on their doorposts. Jesus' atonement grants salvation to all mankind. *Exaltation*, however, comes not from Christ's sacrifice alone, but from our voluntary acceptance of it. As we wholeheartedly accept Jesus as our Savior and follow him, then we can be "justified by his blood [and] saved from wrath through him" (ROMANS 5:9).

Today, Jews use a roasted shankbone, or *Zeroa* (Zeh-ROH-ah), to remind them of the Paschal lamb, which is no longer sacrificed and eaten.

Beitzah. *Beitzah* (BAY-tzah), or a roasted egg, is symbolic of the roasted offering Israelite pilgrims sacrificed at the temple during the three annual Feasts that were held before the temple's destruction. By association, it is a symbol of the temple itself and of mourning for its loss.

Maror. The bitter herb, or *Maror* (Mah-ROR), is a symbol of the Israelites' suffering under the hands of their Egyptian taskmasters. For the Passover meal, horseradish has been the bitter herb of choice for more than four hundred years. Before that, it appears to have been romaine lettuce. The characteristic taste of these "herbs" works wonderfully well as a symbolic reminder of Israel's experience in Egypt. The first taste of romaine lettuce is fairly sweet, but quickly becomes bitter. Horseradish is initially (relatively) mild, but has a pungent aftertaste. Israel was at first welcomed to Egypt. Living there was a blessing for them. When a new Pharaoh came to power and enslaved them, however, life in Egypt became and remained miserable. On a spiritual level, the land of Egypt is symbolic of sin. Sin often appears sweet or mild at first; but all too soon, all that remains are its bitter and overpowering consequences.

Haroset. *Haroset* (Char-RO-set) is a fruit and nut mixture symbolic of the building materials used by Israelite slaves to construct the Egyptian pleasure cities of Pithom and Ramses. The apple and nut pieces represent the clay of the brick; the cinnamon represents the straw added to the mortar; and the wine (or grape juice) represents the blood of the Israelite slaves. Its sweetness promises a better world to come.

Karpas. Parsley, or *Karpas* (KAHR-pahs), which is dipped into a dish of salt water before being eaten, symbolizes the Israelites' new life of freedom. In the past, when green vegetables were difficult to obtain, Eastern European Jews substituted a peeled, boiled potato for the parsley. Many Jewish families still use a potato today. Others use watercress, celery leaves, green onions, or even radishes.

Three Matzot. *Matzah* (the plural form is *Matzot*) is a form of unleavened bread and represents Israel's abrupt and swift escape from Egypt—a flight so sudden that the Israelites could not wait for their bread dough to rise but had to bake it while it was still flat. Leaven causes dough to rise through a unique fermentation process that transforms, or *corrupts*, the original ingredients. Subsequently, gasses are produced that cause the dough to rise. Anciently, leaven was generally associated with the corruption of sin and, specifically, with the inflated self-importance of pride. The use of unleavened bread during the Passover, then, suggests the quick surety of the Lord's redemptive word and at the same time cautions the children of Israel against moral corruption and pride.

The Actual Meal

Unlike the famous bounty of most modern Passover meals, our family has chosen to eat a tasty but relatively simple meal. Instead of elaborate meal preparation, I direct my limited supply of emotional and physical energy toward explaining the important ritual aspects of the Passover meal and toward keeping the children engaged and happy with that. If you prefer a more authentic celebration, however, any Jewish cookbook will provide you with ample recipes for other non-ritual foods that you may wish to eat. If you prefer not to bother with a meal at all, that is also appropriate. Children can learn a lot from simply learning about and tasting the ritual foods.

The Celebration

You may wish to begin your celebration as Jewish people do. As Passover approaches, the house is thoroughly cleaned and all leavening (any product containing yeast) is taken from the house and burned. This prohibition traditionally includes any product containing grain (wheat, barley, oats, spelt, and rye) that has been allowed contact with water for more than eighteen minutes (the time required to begin fermentation) before baking. In strictly observant homes, everyday dishes, silverware, and kitchen tools, if not ritually cleaned beforehand, are also included in the purging. The night before Passover, parents and children recite a set prayer, and the family searches through the darkened house with flashlights (candles or lamps are more fun) for any remaining leavening. Beforehand, however, parents secretly (and strategically) place ten crumbs of the prohibited foods in places where children are able to find them. All ten crumbs must be found, put into a bag, and ceremoniously burned the next morning.

Having symbolically cleansed the home of all corruption and evil, the Passover celebration can properly begin the next day. Even if you choose not to rid your house of all leavening, an excuse to make the family clean up is usually a good idea—a clean house lends a peaceful and orderly tone to the next day's festivities.

Zeroa (Lamb Shankbone)

Independent butcher shops usually stock lamb shanks or stripped shankbones especially for Passover. The in-house butcher of our local grocery store gives away the stripped bones for free during the Passover season. I like to use a bone with a little bit of meat on it and then broil the bone in the oven. It smells wonderful and provides little mouths with delectable snips after the Passover meal.

Matzah (Unleavened Bread)

You can purchase Matzah from the grocery store or try your hand at homemade unleavened bread. Here is a simple recipe:

3 cups flour (or *Matzah* meal)
1/4 teaspoon salt
Water

Preheat oven to 400° F.

Combine flour and salt in a medium-sized bowl. Slowly add enough water so that the dough pulls away from the sides of the bowl and is soft and pliable. Add more flour if the dough becomes too tacky.

Divide dough into three portions. On a floured surface, roll out each portion as you would a piecrust (try to make it thin, but don't worry too much about it—during the Middle Ages unleavened bread was sometimes more than an inch thick).

Roll each sheet of dough onto the rolling pin and then unroll it onto a lightly oiled cookie sheet (vegetable oil is kosher). Without puncturing the dough, prick dough lightly a few times with a fork. Bake immediately until browned, turning once. Carefully slide the three bread rounds from the cookie sheets onto a kitchen towel or rack to cool.

If kept in an airtight container, *Matzah* can be made several days before the Passover meal.

Haroset (Fruit and Nut Mixture)

1/2 cup almonds, finely chopped or ground
1/2 large apple, finely chopped
3 tablespoons grape juice
1/4 teaspoon cinnamon, shaved or powdered
Dried dates, apricots, and figs, finely chopped (optional)
Walnuts or pecans, finely chopped or ground (optional)
Sesame seeds, toasted (optional)
Pinch of ginger, ground (optional)

Mix together the almonds, apple, grape juice, and cinnamon. Add one or more of the optional ingredients. For a more authentic mixture (and some fun for a helper), use a razor blade and shave off small pieces of cinnamon from a cinnamon stick or allow a child to grate the stick in a new pencil sharpener. Next, break the cinnamon shavings into smaller pieces to resemble bits of straw. Make enough to equal 1/4 teaspoon.

Our family likes a chunky *Haroset*, so I chop the nuts and fruit separately and by hand. For *Haroset* with a smoother consistency, use a food processor to grind the almonds to a powder-like consistency and set aside. Combine the apples and other fruit and chop them thoroughly in the food processor. This will look like a pasty mush. Mix the almonds and fruit together, along with enough grape juice to create a desirable consistency.

I always make more *Haroset* than we need because my family loves to eat it the next day on breadsticks dipped in olive oil. Refrigerate all unused portions.

Haroset can be made the day before the Passover meal.

Beitzah (Roasted Egg)

1 large egg, free from cracks

Place the egg in a small pan in a cold oven. Roast the egg at 200° F. for 1½ hours.

Increase oven temperature to 300° F. and roast for ½ hour more. The egg is done when small brown dots appear on the shell. Remove the egg from the oven, cool, and refrigerate until needed.

As a quicker, alternative method, in a small pot, cover an egg and the outer skin of an onion (to color the egg) with cold water. Hard boil the egg. Transfer the hot egg from the pot onto a small pan and broil briefly in the oven. Turn the egg every minute until all areas of the shell are speckled with brown spots. Cool and refrigerate until needed.

The roasted egg can be made several days before the Passover meal.

Maror (Bitter Herb)

It is possible to make fresh horseradish puree. So little is needed, though, that unless your family loves to eat it, just run to the grocery store and buy a small bottle of horseradish puree. For that matter, just run to the grocery store and buy a small head of romaine lettuce instead—it is easier to dip into the *Haroset* than pureed horseradish.

Jerusalem Dinner

At mealtimes, the early Israelites sat on mats around a common bowl of food set on the floor. As their affluence increased, many Israelites adopted the Roman custom of reclining on couches or pillows while eating from low tables—an elbow supporting the upper body, with a pillow under the elbow. This was certainly the custom by the time Jesus was living in Israel. The habit of luxuriating while eating underscored their freedom from slavery. Though food was served on a table instead of the floor, it was still a common practice to have one central bowl of food into which all dipped their hands. Occasionally, however, and certainly for more formal meals, separate portions were set on individual plates. Utensils were not used, but rather, a piece of flat bread was held between the thumb and two fingers and used as a food scoop and a sop for broth. Other foods were eaten with just the fingers. As an understandable custom, hands were washed both before and after a meal.

To create your own Jerusalem dinner, eat by lamp or candlelight and experiment with different kinds of olives, cheeses, dried fruits, and recipes for more complex dishes. Ingredients from the following food list can be mixed and matched to create an interesting and appealing Jerusalem Dinner each year.

Foods of Jesus' Time and Place

Wheat	Peas	Milk	Turmeric
Barley	Beans (Broad)	Butter	Cinnamon
Rye	Garlic	Cheese (soft and hard)	Saffron
Millet	Onions	Yogurt	Mustard
Sesame seeds	Leeks	Honey	Anise
Figs (usually dried)	Carrots	Olive oil	Parsley
Grapes	Cucumbers	Nuts (almonds, pistachios, walnuts)	
Raisins	Greens	Dill	
Dates	Fish (those with fins and scales)	Cumin	
Pomegranates	Chicken	Coriander	
Cantaloupe	Mutton, Lamb	Mint	
Apricots	Beef		
Olives	Eggs		
Lentils			

The preceding list is not exhaustive. Among those things that are missing are beetles and locusts, but this list is certainly enough to put on a meal. We assume Jesus usually ate the light and simple fare of a peasant. The poorer classes rarely ate meat other than during ritualistic meals. And, because it seems to have been principally the kings who owned the groves of nut trees, we can also assume that Jesus ate nuts only on rare occasions. Wine (grape juice), fish, bread, parched grains, lentils, figs, olives, and olive oil are all safe bets when you are choosing authentic foods that Jesus would have eaten.

Here are a few meal ideas:

Simple: Grape juice, broiled fish, whole wheat loaves, dried figs, and goat cheese.

Relatively simple: Grape juice, flat bread, lentil soup, dried figs, dates, olives, and cheese.

More adventurous: Goat's milk, Ezekiel bread, lamb and barley, cucumber salad, melon, honeyed yogurt, and olives.

A local Mediterranean deli, Eastern foods market, or health food store should stock most of the ingredients and ready-made foods listed above that are needed to prepare your own Jerusalem dinner.

Lentil Soup

2 tablespoons olive oil
2 cups onion, chopped
3 carrots, coarsely chopped
$^{3}/_{4}$ teaspoon marjoram, dried
$^{3}/_{4}$ teaspoon thyme, dried
7 cups broth (chicken, beef, or vegetable)
1 pound lentils
$^{1}/_{2}$ teaspoon salt
$^{1}/_{4}$ teaspoon pepper
$^{3}/_{4}$ cup grape juice
2 tablespoons parsley, dried

Sauté onion, carrots, marjoram, and thyme in oil, just until onion is soft. Transfer mixture to a large pot and add broth and lentils. Cover and simmer for 45 minutes to 1 hour (expect the soup to be thick). Add remaining ingredients and simmer for an additional 10 minutes.

Serves 6.

Bulgur and Onion Pilaf

2 tablespoons olive oil
1 cup bulgur, coarsely ground
2 tablespoons olive oil
2 cups red onion, chopped
2 cups chicken stock
$1^{1}/_{2}$ teaspoons coriander, ground
Pinch of cinnamon, ground
1 teaspoon salt
2 teaspoons fresh mint, chopped
Additional salt, to taste

Brown bulgur in olive oil. Set aside. Sauté onion until soft; mix with bulgur. Add chicken stock, coriander, cinnamon, and salt. Bring mixture to a boil, reduce to a low simmer, cover, and cook for 10 minutes. Add mint and salt to taste. Cover and simmer an additional 10 to 12 minutes or until bulgur is tender.

Serves 4 to 6.

Seasoned Lamb and Barley

2 tablespoons butter
1 cup barley, rinsed and drained
1 tablespoon olive oil
3 cloves garlic, crushed
2 medium onions, chopped
1 pound lamb stewing meat, boneless and trimmed of fat, cut into bite-sized pieces
Salt to taste
Pepper to taste
1 tablespoon olive oil
6 cups chicken stock, divided

Preheat oven to 350° F.

Brown barley in butter. Set aside. Sauté garlic and onion in olive oil. Combine barley and onion mixture in a 2-quart casserole dish. Set aside. Sprinkle lamb meat with salt and pepper. Brown in olive oil then place atop barley mixture. Pour 3 cups chicken stock over the meat. Cover and bake for 1 hour, or until the liquid is almost absorbed. Add the remaining chicken stock. Bake for another 50 minutes, or until the meat is tender. Season with salt and pepper to taste.

Serves 6.

Flatbread

If you already own a baker's paddle and baking tiles, now you have an excuse to use them. If not, substitute a 1/4-inch wooden board and an upside down cookie sheet.

1 tablespoon yeast
1 cup lukewarm water
4 cups unbleached white flour
1 cup whole wheat flour
1 teaspoon salt

Preheat oven and baking tiles (or cookie sheet) to 525° F.

Dissolve yeast in water; set aside to proof.

Combine flours and salt. Add yeast mixture and stir. Continue adding extra water until the dough is very stiff.

On a lightly floured surface, knead the dough until it is smooth and elastic (about 5 minutes). Place dough in a greased bowl, cover, and let rise until doubled. Punch down, and mold dough into 6 round pieces about 3 inches in diameter. Be sure to seal the dough by rolling it around in your hands until it is smooth and nearly seamless. Place the dough balls on a tray, cover completely, and let rise for 1 hour.

On a lightly floured surface, roll out one ball of dough into an 8- or 9-inch circle. Place it on a floured baker's paddle (or ¼-inch wooden board) and slide it onto the baking tiles in the oven. While one loaf is baking, roll out the next.

Bake each loaf for 7 to 8 minutes. Very light brown spots will form on the loaf after it has puffed up like a ball. Remove it from the oven and place on a terry-cloth towel. Cover the bread with another towel. Stack the loaves one on top of the other as they come from the oven, always completely covering the stack (this may require more than one towel). Keep the loaves completely covered until cooled.

Makes 6 loaves.

Yogurt

4 cups antibiotic-free milk (2 percent or whole)
1/4 cup active plain yogurt at room temperature (or 2 tablespoons dry yogurt starter)
Honey to taste

Heat milk just below boiling (180° F.). Cool milk slightly (to 110° F.). Combine milk and yogurt and mix thoroughly. Pour yogurt mixture into a glass quart jar and cap the jar with a lid. Set the glass jar in a pot with a lid. Cover ¾ of the jar with warm water and replace lid. Wrap the covered pot with a towel(s) and place it on a heating pad set to medium heat. Let it stand overnight. Refrigerate yogurt before using. Don't forget to take out ¼ cup if you're planning on making it again.

Add honey to sweeten as desired.

Makes 1 quart.

Yogurt Cheese

This simple recipe is similar to cream cheese and is a fun addition to an authentic meal, or any meal for that matter.

Double the yogurt recipe and reserve 1 quart to make into cheese.

Place in a large bowl a 1 1/2 foot square piece of cheesecloth (I use an old dishcloth). Pour 1 quart chilled yogurt into the cloth. Bring up the corners of the cloth and tie them together. Hang this bag above the bowl on the counter overnight or up to 2 days. Season, as desired, with fresh herbs, such as parsley, dill, or garlic.

Makes ¾ cup.

Easter Breakfast Rolls

Prepare these rolls the night before Easter for part of a delicious Easter-morning breakfast.

1 package frozen bread or roll dough, thawed (or use the dough for your favorite homemade rolls)

6 tablespoons sugar
1 teaspoon cinnamon
1 bag large marshmallows
1/4 cup butter, melted

Combine sugar and cinnamon in a small bowl and set aside. Divide the dough into individual roll-sized portions. Press each portion into a flat circle. Place 1 large marshmallow in the center of each roll. Pinch roll dough very firmly around the marshmallow. Roll each into a seamless, or nearly seamless, ball with your hands. Brush rolls with melted butter. Sprinkle sugar mixture over rolls.

Cover rolls with plastic wrap and put in the refrigerator overnight.

On Sunday morning, preheat oven to 350° F.

Take rolls out of the refrigerator and bake for 15 minutes until rolls are golden brown. Just like Christ's tomb on Easter Sunday, these rolls will be empty!

Serving size depends on amount of dough used.

Broiled Fish

Luke records that Jesus ate broiled fish served with honeycomb. You may be in luck and discover a local farmer who keeps bees and is willing to sell you raw honey in the comb. In the event that you can't, most health food stores now sell some form of packaged honeycomb. A one-inch square of honeycomb per person is sufficient for this meal.

2 pounds fish fillets or steaks
(fresh flounder, sole, or tuna)
Olive oil
1 teaspoon fresh parsley, chopped
1 teaspoon green onions, chopped
1 teaspoon fresh dill, chopped
1/4 cup olive oil
Juice of one lemon
Salt and pepper

Brush fish with olive oil. Combine parsley, green onions, and dill. Add 1/4 cup olive oil, lemon, salt, and pepper. Set aside.

Preheat oven broiler. Place fish on a broiler pan placed on the rack closest to the broiling element. Broil fish steaks for 5 minutes on each side and fillets for 2 to 3 minutes each side. During the last minute of cooking, pour the marinade over fish.

Serve with accumulated pan juices.

Serves 6.

Reading for Day 1

Triumphal Entry

MATTHEW 21

1 And when they drew nigh unto Jerusalem, and were come to Bethphage, unto the mount of Olives, then sent Jesus two disciples,

2 Saying unto them, Go into the village over against you, and straightway ye shall find an ass tied, and a colt with her: loose them, and bring them unto me.

3 And if any man say ought unto you, ye shall say, The Lord hath need of them; and straightway he will send them.

4 All this was done, that it might be fulfilled which was spoken by the prophet, saying,

5 Tell ye the daughter of Sion, Behold, thy King cometh unto thee, meek, and sitting upon an ass, and a colt the foal of an ass.

6 And the disciples went, and did as Jesus commanded them,

7 And brought the ass, and the colt, and put on them their clothes, and they set him thereon.

8 And a very great multitude spread their garments in the way; others cut down branches from the trees, and strawed them in the way.

9 And the multitudes that went before, and that followed, cried, saying, Hosanna to the Son of David: Blessed is he that cometh in the name of the Lord; Hosanna in the highest.

10 And when he was come into Jerusalem, all the city was moved, saying, Who is this?

11 And the multitude said, This is Jesus the prophet of Nazareth of Galilee.

MARK 11

1 And when they came nigh to Jerusalem, unto Bethphage and Bethany, at the mount of Olives, he sendeth forth two of his disciples,

2 And saith unto them, Go your way into the village over against you: and as soon as ye be entered into it, ye shall find a colt tied, whereon never man sat; loose him, and bring him.

3 And if any man say unto you, Why do ye this? say ye that the Lord hath need of him; and straightway he will send him hither.

4 And they went their way, and found the colt tied by the door without in a place where two ways met; and they loose him.

5 And certain of them that stood there said unto them, What do ye, loosing the colt?

6 And they said unto them even as Jesus had commanded: and they let them go.

7 And they brought the colt to Jesus, and cast their garments on him; and he sat upon him.

8 And many spread their garments in the way: and others cut down branches off the trees, and strawed them in the way.

9 And they that went before, and they that followed, cried, saying, Hosanna; Blessed is he that cometh in the name of the Lord:

10 Blessed be the kingdom of our father David, that cometh in the name of the Lord: Hosanna in the highest.

LUKE 19

28 And when he had thus spoken, he went before, ascending up to Jerusalem.

29 And it came to pass, when he was come nigh to Bethphage and Bethany, at the mount called the mount of Olives, he sent two of his disciples,

30 Saying, Go ye into the village over against you; in the which at your entering ye shall find a colt tied, whereon yet never man sat: loose him, and bring him hither.

31 And if any man ask you, Why do ye loose him? thus shall ye say unto him, Because the Lord hath need of him.

32 And they that were sent went their way, and found even as he had said unto them.

33 And as they were loosing the colt, the owners thereof said unto them, Why loose ye the colt?

34 And they said, The Lord hath need of him.

35 And they brought him to Jesus: and they cast their garments upon the colt, and they set Jesus thereon.

36 And as he went, they spread their clothes in the way.

37 And when he was come nigh, even now at the descent of the mount of Olives, the whole multitude of the disciples began to rejoice and praise God with a loud voice for all the mighty works that they had seen;

38 Saying, Blessed be the King that cometh in the name of the Lord: peace in heaven, and glory in the highest.

JOHN 12

14 And Jesus, when he had found a young ass, sat thereon; as it is written,

15 Fear not, daughter of Sion: behold, thy King cometh, sitting on an ass's colt.

12 On the next day much people that were come to the feast, when they heard that Jesus was coming to Jerusalem,

13 Took branches of palm trees, and went forth to meet him, and cried, Hosanna: Blessed is the King of Israel that cometh in the name of the Lord.

16 These things understood not his disciples at the first: but when Jesus was glorified, then remembered they that these things were written of him, and that they had done these things unto him.

17 The people therefore that was with him when he called Lazarus out of his grave, and raised him from the dead, bare record.

18 For this cause the people also met him, for that they heard that he had done this miracle.

19 The Pharisees therefore said among themselves,

39 And some of the Pharisees from among the multitude said unto him, Master, rebuke thy disciples.
40 And he answered and said unto them, I tell you that, if these should hold their peace, the stones would immediately cry out.
41 And when he was come near, he beheld the city, and wept over it,
42 Saying, If thou hadst known, even thou, at least in this thy day, the things which belong unto thy peace! but now they are hid from thine eyes.
43 For the days shall come upon thee, that thine enemies shall cast a trench about thee, and compass thee round, and keep thee in on every side,
44 And shall lay thee even with the ground, and thy children within thee; and they shall not leave in thee one stone upon another; because thou knewest not the time of thy visitation.

Perceive ye how ye prevail nothing? behold, the world is gone after him.

20 And there were certain Greeks among them that came up to worship at the feast:
21 The same came therefore to Philip, which was of Bethsaida of Galilee, and desired him, saying, Sir, we would see Jesus.
22 Philip cometh and telleth Andrew: and again Andrew and Philip tell Jesus.
23 And Jesus answered them, saying, The hour is come, that the Son of man should be glorified.
24 Verily, verily, I say unto you, Except a corn of wheat fall into the ground and die, it abideth alone: but if it die, it bringeth forth much fruit.
25 He that loveth his life shall lose it; and he that hateth his life in this world shall keep it unto life eternal.
26 If any man serve me, let him follow me; and where I am, there shall also my servant be: if any man serve me, him will my Father honour.
27 Now is my soul troubled; and what shall I say? Father, save me from this hour: but for this cause came I unto this hour.
28 Father, glorify thy name. Then came there a voice from heaven, saying, I have both glorified it, and will glorify it again.
29 The people therefore, that stood by, and heard it, said that it thundered: others said, An angel spake to him.
30 Jesus answered and said, This voice came not because of me, but for your sakes.
31 Now is the judgment of this world: now shall the prince of this world be cast out.
32 And I, if I be lifted up from the earth, will draw all men unto me.
33 This he said, signifying what death he should die.
34 The people answered him, We have heard out of the law that Christ abideth for ever: and how sayest thou, The Son of man must be lifted up? who is this Son of man?
35 Then Jesus said unto them, Yet a little while is the light with you. Walk while ye have the light, lest darkness come upon you: for he that walketh in darkness knoweth not whither he goeth.
36 While ye have light, believe in the light, that ye may be the children of light. These things spake Jesus, and departed, and did hide himself from them.

Matthew 21	Mark 11	Luke 19	John 12
	11 And Jesus entered into Jerusalem, and into the temple: and when he had looked round about upon all things, and now the eventide was come, he went out unto Bethany with the twelve.		
Reading for Day 2			
	12 And on the morrow, when they were come from Bethany, he was hungry: 13 And seeing a fig tree afar off having leaves, he came, if haply he might find any thing thereon: and when he came to it, he found nothing but leaves; for the time of figs was not yet. 14 And Jesus answered and said unto it, No man eat fruit of thee hereafter for ever. And his disciples heard it.		
Cleansing of the Temple			
12 And Jesus went into the temple of God, and cast out all them that sold and bought in the temple, and overthrew the tables of the moneychangers, and the seats of them that sold doves,	15 And they come to Jerusalem: and Jesus went into the temple, and began to cast out them that sold and bought in the temple, and overthrew the tables of the moneychangers, and the seats of them that sold doves; 16 And would not suffer that any man should carry any vessel through the temple.	45 And he went into the temple, and began to cast out them that sold therein, and them that bought;	
13 And said unto them, It is written, My house shall be called the house of prayer; but ye have made it a den of thieves. 14 And the blind and the lame came to him in the temple; and he healed them. 15 And when the chief priests and scribes saw the wonderful things that he did, and the children crying in the temple, and saying, Hosanna to the Son of David; they were sore displeased, 16 And said unto him, Hearest thou what these say? And Jesus saith unto them, Yea; have ye never read, Out of the mouth of babes and sucklings thou hast perfected praise?	17 And he taught, saying unto them, Is it not written, My house shall be called of all nations the house of prayer? but ye have made it a den of thieves.	46 Saying unto them, It is written, My house is the house of prayer: but ye have made it a den of thieves.	
	18 And the scribes and chief priests heard it, and sought how they might destroy him: for they feared him, because all the people was astonished at his doctrine.	47 And he taught daily in the temple. But the chief priests and the scribes and the chief of the people sought to destroy him, 48 And could not find what they might do: for all the people were very attentive to hear him.	
17 And he left them, and went out of the city into Bethany; and he lodged there.	19 And when even was come, he went out of the city.		
Reading for Days 3 and 4			
18 Now in the morning as he returned into the city, he hungered. 19 And when he saw a fig tree in the way, he came to it, and found nothing thereon, but leaves only, and said unto it, Let no fruit grow on thee henceforward for ever. And presently the fig tree withered away.			

20 And when the disciples saw it, they marvelled, saying, How soon is the fig tree withered away!

21 Jesus answered and said unto them, Verily I say unto you, If ye have faith, and doubt not, ye shall not only do this which is done to the fig tree, but also if ye shall say unto this mountain, Be thou removed, and be thou cast into the sea; it shall be done.

22 And all things, whatsoever ye shall ask in prayer, believing, ye shall receive.

20 And in the morning, as they passed by, they saw the fig tree dried up from the roots.

21 And Peter calling to remembrance saith unto him, Master, behold, the fig tree which thou cursedst is withered away.

22 And Jesus answering saith unto them, Have faith in God.

23 For verily I say unto you, That whosoever shall say unto this mountain, Be thou removed, and be thou cast into the sea; and shall not doubt in his heart, but shall believe that those things which he saith shall come to pass; he shall have whatsoever he saith.

24 Therefore I say unto you, What things soever ye desire, when ye pray, believe that ye receive them, and ye shall have them.

25 And when ye stand praying, forgive, if ye have ought against any: that your Father also which is in heaven may forgive you your trespasses.

26 But if ye do not forgive, neither will your Father which is in heaven forgive your trespasses.

Jewish Leaders Question Christ's Authority

23 And when he was come into the temple, the chief priests and the elders of the people came unto him as he was teaching, and said, By what authority doest thou these things? and who gave thee this authority?

24 And Jesus answered and said unto them, I also will ask you one thing, which if ye tell me, I in like wise will tell you by what authority I do these things.

25 The baptism of John, whence was it? from heaven, or of men? And they reasoned with themselves, saying, If we shall say, From heaven; he will say unto us, Why did ye not then believe him?

26 But if we shall say, Of men; we fear the people; for all hold John as a prophet.

27 And they answered Jesus, and said, We cannot tell. And he said unto them, Neither tell I you by what authority I do these things.

27 And they come again to Jerusalem: and as he was walking in the temple, there come to him the chief priests, and the scribes, and the elders,

28 And say unto him, By what authority doest thou these things? and who gave thee this authority to do these things?

29 And Jesus answered and said unto them, I will also ask of you one question, and answer me, and I will tell you by what authority I do these things.

30 The baptism of John, was it from heaven, or of men? answer me.

31 And they reasoned with themselves, saying, If we shall say, From heaven; he will say, Why then did ye not believe him?

32 But if we shall say, Of men; they feared the people: for all men counted John, that he was a prophet indeed.

33 And they answered and said unto Jesus, We cannot tell. And Jesus answering saith unto them, Neither do I tell you by what authority I do these things.

CHAPTER 20

1 And it came to pass, that on one of those days, as he taught the people in the temple, and preached the gospel, the chief priests and the scribes came upon him with the elders,

2 And spake unto him, saying, Tell us, by what authority doest thou these things? or who is he that gave thee this authority?

3 And he answered and said unto them, I will also ask you one thing; and answer me:

4 The baptism of John, was it from heaven, or of men?

5 And they reasoned with themselves, saying, If we shall say, From heaven; he will say, Why then believed ye him not?

6 But and if we say, Of men; all the people will stone us: for they be persuaded that John was a prophet.

7 And they answered, that they could not tell whence it was.

8 And Jesus said unto them, Neither tell I you by what authority I do these things.

Parable: Two Sons

28 But what think ye? A certain man had two sons; and he came to the first, and said, Son, go work to day in my vineyard.

29 He answered and said, I will not: but afterward he repented, and went.

30 And he came to the second, and said likewise. And he answered and said, I go, sir: and went not.

31 Whether of them twain did the will of his father? They say unto him, The first. Jesus saith unto them, Verily I say unto you, That the publicans and the harlots go into the kingdom of God before you.

Matthew 21

32 For John came unto you in the way of righteousness, and ye believed him not: but the publicans and the harlots believed him: and ye, when ye had seen it, repented not afterward, that ye might believe him.

PARABLE: THE WICKED HUSBANDMEN

Matthew 21

33 Hear another parable: There was a certain householder, which planted a vineyard, and hedged it round about, and digged a winepress in it, and built a tower, and let it out to husbandmen, and went into a far country:

34 And when the time of the fruit drew near, he sent his servants to the husbandmen, that they might receive the fruits of it.

35 And the husbandmen took his servants, and beat one, and killed another, and stoned another.

36 Again, he sent other servants more than the first: and they did unto them likewise.

37 But last of all he sent unto them his son, saying, They will reverence my son.

38 But when the husbandmen saw the son, they said among themselves, This is the heir; come, let us kill him, and let us seize on his inheritance.

39 And they caught him, and cast him out of the vineyard, and slew him.

40 When the lord therefore of the vineyard cometh, what will he do unto those husbandmen?

41 They say unto him, He will miserably destroy those wicked men, and will let out his vineyard unto other husbandmen, which shall render him the fruits in their seasons.

42 Jesus saith unto them, Did ye never read in the scriptures, The stone which the builders rejected, the same is become the head of the corner: this is the Lord's doing, and it is marvellous in our eyes?

43 Therefore say I unto you, The kingdom of God shall be taken from you, and given to a nation bringing forth the fruits thereof.

44 And whosoever shall fall on this stone shall be broken: but on whomsoever it shall fall, it will grind him to powder.

45 And when the chief priests and Pharisees had heard his parables, they perceived that he spake of them.

46 But when they sought to lay hands on him, they feared the multitude, because they took him for a prophet.

Mark 12

CHAPTER 12

1 And he began to speak unto them by parables. A certain man planted a vineyard, and set an hedge about it, and digged a place for the winefat, and built a tower, and let it out to husbandmen, and went into a far country.

2 And at the season he sent to the husbandmen a servant, that he might receive from the husbandmen of the fruit of the vineyard.

3 And they caught him, and beat him, and sent him away empty.

4 And again he sent unto them another servant; and at him they cast stones, and wounded him in the head, and sent him away shamefully handled.

5 And again he sent another; and him they killed, and many others; beating some, and killing some.

6 Having yet therefore one son, his wellbeloved, he sent him also last unto them, saying, They will reverence my son.

7 But those husbandmen said among themselves, This is the heir; come, let us kill him, and the inheritance shall be ours.

8 And they took him, and killed him, and cast him out of the vineyard.

9 What shall therefore the lord of the vineyard do? he will come and destroy the husbandmen, and will give the vineyard unto others.

10 And have ye not read this scripture; The stone which the builders rejected is become the head of the corner:

11 This was the Lord's doing, and it is marvellous in our eyes?

12 And they sought to lay hold on him, but feared the people: for they knew that he had spoken the parable against them: and they left him, and went their way.

Luke 20

9 Then began he to speak to the people this parable; A certain man planted a vineyard, and let it forth to husbandmen, and went into a far country for a long time.

10 And at the season he sent a servant to the husbandmen, that they should give him of the fruit of the vineyard: but the husbandmen beat him, and sent him away empty.

11 And again he sent another servant: and they beat him also, and entreated him shamefully, and sent him away empty.

12 And again he sent a third: and they wounded him also, and cast him out.

13 Then said the lord of the vineyard, What shall I do? I will send my beloved son: it may be they will reverence him when they see him.

14 But when the husbandmen saw him, they reasoned among themselves, saying, This is the heir: come, let us kill him, that the inheritance may be ours.

15 So they cast him out of the vineyard, and killed him. What therefore shall the lord of the vineyard do unto them?

16 He shall come and destroy these husbandmen, and shall give the vineyard to others. And when they heard it, they said, God forbid.

17 And he beheld them, and said, What is this then that is written, The stone which the builders rejected, the same is become the head of the corner?

18 Whosoever shall fall upon that stone shall be broken; but on whomsoever it shall fall, it will grind him to powder.

PARABLE: THE MARRIAGE OF THE KING'S SON

Matthew 22

CHAPTER 22

1 And Jesus answered and spake unto them again by parables, and said,

2 The kingdom of heaven is like unto a certain king, which made a marriage for his son,

3 And sent forth his servants to call them that were bidden to the wedding: and they would not come.
4 Again, he sent forth other servants, saying, Tell them which are bidden, Behold, I have prepared my dinner: my oxen and my fatlings are killed, and all things are ready: come unto the marriage.
5 But they made light of it, and went their ways, one to his farm, another to his merchandise:
6 And the remnant took his servants, and entreated them spitefully, and slew them.
7 But when the king heard thereof, he was wroth: and he sent forth his armies, and destroyed those murderers, and burned up their city.
8 Then saith he to his servants, The wedding is ready, but they which were bidden were not worthy.
9 Go ye therefore into the highways, and as many as ye shall find, bid to the marriage.
10 So those servants went out into the highways, and gathered together all as many as they found, both bad and good: and the wedding was furnished with guests.
11 And when the king came in to see the guests, he saw there a man which had not on a wedding garment:
12 And he saith unto him, Friend, how camest thou in hither not having a wedding garment? And he was speechless.
13 Then said the king to the servants, Bind him hand and foot, and take him away, and cast him into outer darkness; there shall be weeping and gnashing of teeth.
14 For many are called, but few are chosen.

Pharisees and Herodians Challenge Christ

15 Then went the Pharisees, and took counsel how they might entangle him in his talk.

16 And they sent out unto him their disciples with the Herodians, saying, Master, we know that thou art true, and teachest the way of God in truth, neither carest thou for any man: for thou regardest not the person of men.
17 Tell us therefore, What thinkest thou? Is it lawful to give tribute unto Caesar, or not?

18 But Jesus perceived their wickedness, and said, Why tempt ye me, ye hypocrites?
19 Shew me the tribute money. And they brought unto him a penny.
20 And he saith unto them, Whose is this image and superscription?

21 They say unto him, Caesar's. Then saith he unto them, Render therefore unto Caesar the things which are Caesar's; and unto God the things that are God's.
22 When they had heard these words, they marvelled, and left him, and went their way.

13 And they send unto him certain of the Pharisees and of the Herodians, to catch him in his words.
14 And when they were come, they say unto him, Master, we know that thou art true, and carest for no man: for thou regardest not the person of men, but teachest the way of God in truth: Is it lawful to give tribute to Caesar, or not?

15 Shall we give, or shall we not give? But he, knowing their hypocrisy, said unto them, Why tempt ye me? bring me a penny, that I may see it.

16 And they brought it. And he saith unto them, Whose is this image and superscription? And they said unto him, Caesar's.
17 And Jesus answering said unto them, Render to Caesar the things that are Caesar's, and to God the things that are God's. And they marvelled at him.

19 And the chief priests and the scribes the same hour sought to lay hands on him; and they feared the people: for they perceived that he had spoken this parable against them.
20 And they watched him, and sent forth spies, which should feign themselves just men, that they might take hold of his words, that so they might deliver him unto the power and authority of the governor.
21 And they asked him, saying, Master, we know that thou sayest and teachest rightly, neither acceptest thou the person of any, but teachest the way of God truly:
22 Is it lawful for us to give tribute unto Caesar, or no?
23 But he perceived their craftiness, and said unto them, Why tempt ye me?

24 Shew me a penny. Whose image and superscription hath it? They answered and said, Caesar's.

25 And he said unto them, Render therefore unto Caesar the things which be Caesar's, and unto God the things which be God's.
26 And they could not take hold of his words before the people: and they marvelled at his answer, and held their peace.

SADDUCEES CHALLENGE CHRIST

Matthew 22

23 The same day came to him the Sadducees, which say that there is no resurrection, and asked him,
24 Saying, Master, Moses said, If a man die, having no children, his brother shall marry his wife, and raise up seed unto his brother.

25 Now there were with us seven brethren: and the first, when he had married a wife, deceased, and, having no issue, left his wife unto his brother:
26 Likewise the second also, and the third, unto the seventh.
27 And last of all the woman died also.

28 Therefore in the resurrection whose wife shall she be of the seven? for they all had her.

29 Jesus answered and said unto them, Ye do err, not knowing the scriptures, nor the power of God.
30 For in the resurrection they neither marry, nor are given in marriage, but are as the angels of God in heaven.
31 But as touching the resurrection of the dead, have ye not read that which was spoken unto you by God, saying,

32 I am the God of Abraham, and the God of Isaac, and the God of Jacob? God is not the God of the dead, but of the living.

33 And when the multitude heard this, they were astonished at his doctrine.

Mark 12

18 Then come unto him the Sadducees, which say there is no resurrection; and they asked him, saying,
19 Master, Moses wrote unto us, If a man's brother die, and leave his wife behind him, and leave no children, that his brother should take his wife, and raise up seed unto his brother.
20 Now there were seven brethren: and the first took a wife, and dying left no seed.

21 And the second took her, and died, neither left he any seed: and the third likewise.
22 And the seven had her, and left no seed: last of all the woman died also.

23 In the resurrection therefore, when they shall rise, whose wife shall she be of them? for the seven had her to wife.
24 And Jesus answering said unto them, Do ye not therefore err, because ye know not the scriptures, neither the power of God?
25 For when they shall rise from the dead, they neither marry, nor are given in marriage; but are as the angels which are in heaven.

26 And as touching the dead, that they rise: have ye not read in the book of Moses, how in the bush God spake unto him, saying, I am the God of Abraham, and the God of Isaac, and the God of Jacob?
27 He is not the God of the dead, but the God of the living: ye therefore do greatly err.

Luke 20

27 Then came to him certain of the Sadducees, which deny that there is any resurrection; and they asked him,
28 Saying, Master, Moses wrote unto us, If any man's brother die, having a wife, and he die without children, that his brother should take his wife, and raise up seed unto his brother.
29 There were therefore seven brethren: and the first took a wife, and died without children.

30 And the second took her to wife, and he died childless.
31 And the third took her; and in like manner the seven also: and they left no children, and died.
32 Last of all the woman died also.
33 Therefore in the resurrection whose wife of them is she? for seven had her to wife.

34 And Jesus answering said unto them, The children of this world marry, and are given in marriage:
35 But they which shall be accounted worthy to obtain that world, and the resurrection from the dead, neither marry, nor are given in marriage:
36 Neither can they die any more: for they are equal unto the angels; and are the children of God, being the children of the resurrection.
37 Now that the dead are raised, even Moses shewed at the bush, when he calleth the Lord the God of Abraham, and the God of Isaac, and the God of Jacob.

38 For he is not a God of the dead, but of the living: for all live unto him.

39 Then certain of the scribes answering said, Master, thou hast well said.
40 And after that they durst not ask him any question at all.

THE GREAT COMMANDMENT

Matthew 22

34 But when the Pharisees had heard that he had put the Sadducees to silence, they were gathered together.
35 Then one of them, which was a lawyer, asked him a question, tempting him, and saying,
36 Master, which is the great commandment in the law?

37 Jesus said unto him, Thou shalt love the Lord thy God with all thy heart, and with all thy soul, and with all thy mind.
38 This is the first and great commandment.
39 And the second is like unto it, Thou shalt love thy neighbour as thyself.
40 On these two commandments hang all the law and the prophets.

Mark 12

28 And one of the scribes came, and having heard them reasoning together, and perceiving that he had answered them well, asked him, Which is the first commandment of all?
29 And Jesus answered him, The first of all the commandments is, Hear, O Israel; The Lord our God is one Lord:
30 And thou shalt love the Lord thy God with all thy heart, and with all thy soul, and with all thy mind, and with all thy strength: this is the first commandment.

31 And the second is like, namely this, Thou shalt love thy neighbour as thyself. There is none other commandment greater than these.

41 While the Pharisees were gathered together, Jesus
asked them,
42 Saying, What think ye of Christ? whose son is he?
They say unto him, The Son of David.
43 He saith unto them, How then doth David in spirit
call him Lord, saying,
44 The Lord said unto my Lord, Sit thou on my right
hand, till I make thine enemies thy footstool?
45 If David then call him Lord, how is he his son?
46 And no man was able to answer him a word, neither
durst any man from that day forth ask him any more ques-
tions.

32 And the scribe said unto him, Well, Master, thou hast
said the truth: for there is one God; and there is none
other but he:
33 And to love him with all the heart, and with all the
understanding, and with all the soul, and with all the
strength, and to love his neighbour as himself, is more than
all whole burnt offerings and sacrifices.
34 And when Jesus saw that he answered discreetly, he
said unto him, Thou art not far from the kingdom of God.
And no man after that durst ask him any question.
35 And Jesus answered and said, while he taught in the
temple, How say the scribes that Christ is the Son of
David?

36 For David himself said by the Holy Ghost, The Lord
said to my Lord, Sit thou on my right hand, till I make
thine enemies thy footstool.

37 David therefore himself calleth him Lord; and
whence is he then his son? And the common people heard
him gladly.

41 And he said unto them, How say they that Christ is
David's son?

42 And David himself saith in the book of Psalms, The
Lord said unto my Lord, Sit thou on my right hand,
43 Till I make thine enemies thy footstool.

44 David therefore calleth him Lord, how is he then his
son?

Condemnation of Hypocrisy

CHAPTER 23

1 Then spake Jesus to the multitude, and to his dis-
ciples,
2 Saying, The scribes and the Pharisees sit in Moses' seat:
3 All therefore whatsoever they bid you observe, that
observe and do; but do not ye after their works: for they
say, and do not.
4 For they bind heavy burdens and grievous to be borne,
and lay them on men's shoulders; but they themselves will
not move them with one of their fingers.
5 But all their works they do for to be seen of men: they
make broad their phylacteries, and enlarge the borders of
their garments,
6 And love the uppermost rooms at feasts, and the chief
seats in the synagogues,
7 And greetings in the markets, and to be called of men,
Rabbi, Rabbi.
8 But be not ye called Rabbi: for one is your Master, even
Christ; and all ye are brethren.
9 And call no man your father upon the earth: for one is
your Father, which is in heaven.
10 Neither be ye called masters: for one is your Master,
even Christ.
11 But he that is greatest among you shall be your ser-
vant.
12 And whosoever shall exalt himself shall be abased;
and he that shall humble himself shall be exalted.
13 But woe unto you, scribes and Pharisees, hypocrites!
for ye shut up the kingdom of heaven against men: for ye
neither go in yourselves, neither suffer ye them that are
entering to go in.
14 Woe unto you, scribes and Pharisees, hypocrites! for
ye devour widows' houses, and for a pretence make long
prayer: therefore ye shall receive the greater damnation.
15 Woe unto you, scribes and Pharisees, hypocrites! for
ye compass sea and land to make one proselyte, and when

38 And he said unto them in his doctrine, Beware of the
scribes, which love to go in long clothing, and love saluta-
tions in the marketplaces,

39 And the chief seats in the synagogues, and the upper-
most rooms at feasts:

40 Which devour widows' houses, and for a pretence
make long prayers: these shall receive greater damnation.

45 Then in the audience of all the people he said unto
his disciples,
46 Beware of the scribes, which desire to walk in long
robes, and love greetings in the markets, and the highest
seats in the synagogues, and the chief rooms at feasts;

47 Which devour widows' houses, and for a shew make
long prayers: the same shall receive greater damnation.

he is made, ye make him twofold more the child of hell
than yourselves.
16 Woe unto you, ye blind guides, which say, Whosoever
shall swear by the temple, it is nothing; but whosoever
shall swear by the gold of the temple, he is a debtor!
17 Ye fools and blind: for whether is greater, the gold, or
the temple that sanctifieth the gold?
18 And, Whosoever shall swear by the altar, it is noth-
ing; but whosoever sweareth by the gift that is upon it, he
is guilty.
19 Ye fools and blind: for whether is greater, the gift, or
the altar that sanctifieth the gift?
20 Whoso therefore shall swear by the altar, sweareth by
it, and by all things thereon.
21 And whoso shall swear by the temple, sweareth by it,
and by him that dwelleth therein.
22 And he that shall swear by heaven, sweareth by the
throne of God, and by him that sitteth thereon.
23 Woe unto you, scribes and Pharisees, hypocrites! for
ye pay tithe of mint and anise and cummin, and have
omitted the weightier matters of the law, judgment, mercy,
and faith: these ought ye to have done, and not to leave
the other undone.
24 Ye blind guides, which strain at a gnat, and swallow a
camel.
25 Woe unto you, scribes and Pharisees, hypocrites! for
ye make clean the outside of the cup and of the platter, but
within they are full of extortion and excess.
26 Thou blind Pharisee, cleanse first that which is within
the cup and platter, that the outside of them may be clean
also.
27 Woe unto you, scribes and Pharisees, hypocrites! for
ye are like unto whited sepulchres, which indeed appear
beautiful outward, but are within full of dead men's bones,
and of all uncleanness.
28 Even so ye also outwardly appear righteous unto men,
but within ye are full of hypocrisy and iniquity.
29 Woe unto you, scribes and Pharisees, hypocrites!
because ye build the tombs of the prophets, and garnish
the sepulchres of the righteous,
30 And say, If we had been in the days of our fathers, we
would not have been partakers with them in the blood of
the prophets.
31 Wherefore ye be witnesses unto yourselves, that ye
are the children of them which killed the prophets.
32 Fill ye up then the measure of your fathers.
33 Ye serpents, ye generation of vipers, how can ye
escape the damnation of hell?
34 Wherefore, behold, I send unto you prophets, and
wise men, and scribes: and some of them ye shall kill and
crucify; and some of them shall ye scourge in your syna-
gogues, and persecute them from city to city:
35 That upon you may come all the righteous blood shed
upon the earth, from the blood of righteous Abel unto the
blood of Zacharias son of Barachias, whom ye slew
between the temple and the altar.
36 Verily I say unto you, All these things shall come
upon this generation.

37 O Jerusalem, Jerusalem, thou that killest the prophets, and stonest them which are sent unto thee, how often would I have gathered thy children together, even as a hen gathereth her chickens under her wings, and ye would not!
38 Behold, your house is left unto you desolate.
39 For I say unto you, Ye shall not see me henceforth, till ye shall say, Blessed is he that cometh in the name of the Lord.

WIDOW'S MITE

41 And Jesus sat over against the treasury, and beheld how the people cast money into the treasury: and many that were rich cast in much.
42 And there came a certain poor widow, and she threw in two mites, which make a farthing.
43 And he called unto him his disciples, and saith unto them, Verily I say unto you, That this poor widow hath cast more in, than all they which have cast into the treasury:
44 For all they did cast in of their abundance; but she of her want did cast in all that she had, even all her living.

CHAPTER 21

1 And he looked up, and saw the rich men casting their gifts into the treasury.
2 And he saw also a certain poor widow casting in thither two mites.
3 And he said, Of a truth I say unto you, that this poor widow hath cast in more than they all:
4 For all these have of their abundance cast in unto the offerings of God: but she of her penury hath cast in all the living that she had.

CHRIST SENT BY THE FATHER

37 But though he had done so many miracles before them, yet they believed not on him:
38 That the saying of Esaias the prophet might be fulfilled, which he spake, Lord, who hath believed our report? and to whom hath the arm of the Lord been revealed?
39 Therefore they could not believe, because that Esaias said again,
40 He hath blinded their eyes, and hardened their heart; that they should not see with their eyes, nor understand with their heart, and be converted, and I should heal them.
41 These things said Esaias, when he saw his glory, and spake of him.
42 Nevertheless among the chief rulers also many believed on him; but because of the Pharisees they did not confess him, lest they should be put out of the synagogue:
43 For they loved the praise of men more than the praise of God.
44 Jesus cried and said, He that believeth on me, believeth not on me, but on him that sent me.
45 And he that seeth me seeth him that sent me.
46 I am come a light into the world, that whosoever believeth on me should not abide in darkness.
47 And if any man hear my words, and believe not, I judge him not: for I came not to judge the world, but to save the world.
48 He that rejecteth me, and receiveth not my words, hath one that judgeth him: the word that I have spoken, the same shall judge him in the last day.
49 For I have not spoken of myself; but the Father which sent me, he gave me a commandment, what I should say, and what I should speak.

John 12

50 And I know that his commandment is life everlast-
ing: whatsoever I speak therefore, even as the Father said
unto me, so I speak.

Olivet Discourse—Signs of the Second Coming

Matthew 24

CHAPTER 24

1 And Jesus went out, and departed from the temple:
and his disciples came to him for to shew him the build-
ings of the temple.
2 And Jesus said unto them, See ye not all these things?
verily I say unto you, There shall not be left here one stone
upon another, that shall not be thrown down.
3 And as he sat upon the mount of Olives, the disciples
came unto him privately, saying, Tell us, when shall these
things be? and what shall be the sign of thy coming, and of
the end of the world?

4 And Jesus answered and said unto them, Take heed
that no man deceive you.
5 For many shall come in my name, saying, I am Christ;
and shall deceive many.
6 And ye shall hear of wars and rumours of wars: see that
ye be not troubled: for all these things must come to pass,
but the end is not yet.
7 For nation shall rise against nation, and kingdom
against kingdom: and there shall be famines, and pesti-
lences, and earthquakes, in divers places.
8 All these are the beginning of sorrows.
9 Then shall they deliver you up to be afflicted, and shall
kill you: and ye shall be hated of all nations for my name's
sake.

10 And then shall many be offended, and shall betray
one another, and shall hate one another.

11 And many false prophets shall rise, and shall deceive
many.
12 And because iniquity shall abound, the love of many
shall wax cold.
13 But he that shall endure unto the end, the same shall
be saved.

14 And this gospel of the kingdom shall be preached in
all the world for a witness unto all nations; and then shall
the end come.

Mark 13

CHAPTER 13

1 And as he went out of the temple, one of his disciples
saith unto him, Master, see what manner of stones and
what buildings are here!
2 And Jesus answering said unto him, Seest thou these
great buildings? there shall not be left one stone upon
another, that shall not be thrown down.
3 And as he sat upon the mount of Olives over against
the temple, Peter and James and John and Andrew asked
him privately,
4 Tell us, when shall these things be? and what shall be
the sign when all these things shall be fulfilled?
5 And Jesus answering them began to say, Take heed lest
any man deceive you:
6 For many shall come in my name, saying, I am Christ;
and shall deceive many.
7 And when ye shall hear of wars and rumours of wars,
be ye not troubled: for such things must needs be; but the
end shall not be yet.
8 For nation shall rise against nation, and kingdom
against kingdom: and there shall be earthquakes in divers
places, and there shall be famines and troubles: these are
the beginnings of sorrows.
9 But take heed to yourselves: for they shall deliver you
up to councils; and in the synagogues ye shall be beaten:
and ye shall be brought before rulers and kings for my sake,
for a testimony against them.
10 And the gospel must first be published among all
nations.
11 But when they shall lead you, and deliver you up,
take no thought beforehand what ye shall speak, neither
do ye premeditate: but whatsoever shall be given you in
that hour, that speak ye: for it is not ye that speak, but the
Holy Ghost.
12 Now the brother shall betray the brother to death,
and the father the son; and children shall rise up against
their parents, and shall cause them to be put to death.

13 And ye shall be hated of all men for my name's sake:
but he that shall endure unto the end, the same shall be
saved.

Luke 21

5 And as some spake of the temple, how it was adorned
with goodly stones and gifts, he said,

6 As for these things which ye behold, the days will
come, in the which there shall not be left one stone upon
another, that shall not be thrown down.
7 And they asked him, saying, Master, but when shall
these things be? and what sign will there be when these
things shall come to pass?

8 And he said, Take heed that ye be not deceived: for
many shall come in my name, saying, I am Christ; and the
time draweth near: go ye not therefore after them.
9 But when ye shall hear of wars and commotions, be
not terrified: for these things must first come to pass; but
the end is not by and by.
10 Then said he unto them, Nation shall rise against
nation, and kingdom against kingdom:
11 And great earthquakes shall be in divers places, and
famines, and pestilences; and fearful sights and great signs
shall there be from heaven.
12 But before all these, they shall lay their hands on you,
and persecute you, delivering you up to the synagogues,
and into prisons, being brought before kings and rulers for
my name's sake.
13 And it shall turn to you for a testimony.

14 Settle it therefore in your hearts, not to meditate
before what ye shall answer:
15 For I will give you a mouth and wisdom, which all
your adversaries shall not be able to gainsay nor resist.

16 And ye shall be betrayed both by parents, and
brethren, and kinsfolks, and friends; and some of you shall
they cause to be put to death.

17 And ye shall be hated of all men for my name's sake.

18 But there shall not an hair of your head perish.
19 In your patience possess ye your souls.

15 When ye therefore shall see the abomination of desolation, spoken of by Daniel the prophet, stand in the holy place, (whoso readeth, let him understand:) 16 Then let them which be in Judaea flee into the mountains:	14 But when ye shall see the abomination of desolation, spoken of by Daniel the prophet, standing where it ought not, (let him that readeth understand,) then let them that be in Judaea flee to the mountains:	20 And when ye shall see Jerusalem compassed with armies, then know that the desolation thereof is nigh. 21 Then let them which are in Judaea flee to the mountains; and let them which are in the midst of it depart out; and let not them that are in the countries enter thereinto. 22 For these be the days of vengeance, that all things which are written may be fulfilled.
17 Let him which is on the housetop not come down to take any thing out of his house:	15 And let him that is on the housetop not go down into the house, neither enter therein, to take any thing out of his house:	
18 Neither let him which is in the field return back to take his clothes.	16 And let him that is in the field not turn back again for to take up his garment.	
19 And woe unto them that are with child, and to them that give suck in those days!	17 But woe to them that are with child, and to them that give suck in those days!	23 But woe unto them that are with child, and to them that give suck, in those days! for there shall be great distress in the land, and wrath upon this people.
20 But pray ye that your flight be not in the winter, neither on the sabbath day:	18 And pray ye that your flight be not in the winter.	
		24 And they shall fall by the edge of the sword, and shall be led away captive into all nations: and Jerusalem shall be trodden down of the Gentiles, until the times of the Gentiles be fulfilled.
21 For then shall be great tribulation, such as was not since the beginning of the world to this time, no, nor ever shall be. 22 And except those days should be shortened, there should no flesh be saved: but for the elect's sake those days shall be shortened. 23 Then if any man shall say unto you, Lo, here is Christ, or there; believe it not. 24 For there shall arise false Christs, and false prophets, and shall shew great signs and wonders; insomuch that, if it were possible, they shall deceive the very elect. 25 Behold, I have told you before. 26 Wherefore if they shall say unto you, Behold, he is in the desert; go not forth: behold, he is in the secret chambers; believe it not. 27 For as the lightning cometh out of the east, and shineth even unto the west; so shall also the coming of the Son of man be. 28 For wheresoever the carcase is, there will the eagles be gathered together.	19 For in those days shall be affliction, such as was not from the beginning of the creation which God created unto this time, neither shall be. 20 And except that the Lord had shortened those days, no flesh should be saved: but for the elect's sake, whom he hath chosen, he hath shortened the days. 21 And then if any man shall say to you, Lo, here is Christ; or, lo, he is there; believe him not: 22 For false Christs and false prophets shall rise, and shall shew signs and wonders, to seduce, if it were possible, even the elect. 23 But take ye heed: behold, I have foretold you all things.	
29 Immediately after the tribulation of those days shall the sun be darkened, and the moon shall not give her light, and the stars shall fall from heaven, and the powers of the heavens shall be shaken:	24 But in those days, after that tribulation, the sun shall be darkened, and the moon shall not give her light, 25 And the stars of heaven shall fall, and the powers that are in heaven shall be shaken.	25 And there shall be signs in the sun, and in the moon, and in the stars; and upon the earth distress of nations, with perplexity; the sea and the waves roaring;
		26 Men's hearts failing them for fear, and for looking after those things which are coming on the earth: for the powers of heaven shall be shaken.
30 And then shall appear the sign of the Son of man in heaven: and then shall all the tribes of the earth mourn, and they shall see the Son of man coming in the clouds of heaven with power and great glory.	26 And then shall they see the Son of man coming in the clouds with great power and glory.	27 And then shall they see the Son of man coming in a cloud with power and great glory.
31 And he shall send his angels with a great sound of a trumpet, and they shall gather together his elect from the four winds, from one end of heaven to the other.	27 And then shall he send his angels, and shall gather together his elect from the four winds, from the uttermost part of the earth to the uttermost part of heaven.	
		28 And when these things begin to come to pass, then look up, and lift up your heads; for your redemption draweth nigh.

Matthew 24

32 Now learn a parable of the fig tree; When his branch is yet tender, and putteth forth leaves, ye know that summer is nigh:

33 So likewise ye, when ye shall see all these things, know that it is near, even at the doors.

34 Verily I say unto you, This generation shall not pass, till all these things be fulfilled.

35 Heaven and earth shall pass away, but my words shall not pass away.

36 But of that day and hour knoweth no man, no, not the angels of heaven, but my Father only.

37 But as the days of Noe were, so shall also the coming of the Son of man be.

38 For as in the days that were before the flood they were eating and drinking, marrying and giving in marriage, until the day that Noe entered into the ark,

39 And knew not until the flood came, and took them all away; so shall also the coming of the Son of man be.

40 Then shall two be in the field; the one shall be taken, and the other left.

41 Two women shall be grinding at the mill; the one shall be taken, and the other left.

42 Watch therefore: for ye know not what hour your Lord doth come.

43 But know this, that if the goodman of the house had known in what watch the thief would come, he would have watched, and would not have suffered his house to be broken up.

44 Therefore be ye also ready: for in such an hour as ye think not the Son of man cometh.

45 Who then is a faithful and wise servant, whom his lord hath made ruler over his household, to give them meat in due season?

46 Blessed is that servant, whom his lord when he cometh shall find so doing.

47 Verily I say unto you, That he shall make him ruler over all his goods.

48 But and if that evil servant shall say in his heart, My lord delayeth his coming;

49 And shall begin to smite his fellowservants, and to eat and drink with the drunken;

50 The lord of that servant shall come in a day when he looketh not for him, and in an hour that he is not aware of,

51 And shall cut him asunder, and appoint him his portion with the hypocrites: there shall be weeping and gnashing of teeth.

Mark 13

28 Now learn a parable of the fig tree; When her branch is yet tender, and putteth forth leaves, ye know that summer is near:

29 So ye in like manner, when ye shall see these things come to pass, know that it is nigh, even at the doors.

30 Verily I say unto you, that this generation shall not pass, till all these things be done.

31 Heaven and earth shall pass away: but my words shall not pass away.

32 But of that day and that hour knoweth no man, no, not the angels which are in heaven, neither the Son, but the Father.

33 Take ye heed, watch and pray: for ye know not when the time is.

34 For the Son of man is as a man taking a far journey, who left his house, and gave authority to his servants, and to every man his work, and commanded the porter to watch.

Luke 21

29 And he spake to them a parable; Behold the fig tree, and all the trees;

30 When they now shoot forth, ye see and know of your own selves that summer is now nigh at hand.

31 So likewise ye, when ye see these things come to pass, know ye that the kingdom of God is nigh at hand.

32 Verily I say unto you, This generation shall not pass away, till all be fulfilled.

33 Heaven and earth shall pass away: but my words shall not pass away.

34 And take heed to yourselves, lest at any time your hearts be overcharged with surfeiting, and drunkenness, and cares of this life, and so that day come upon you unawares.

35 For as a snare shall it come on all them that dwell on the face of the whole earth.

36 Watch ye therefore, and pray always, that ye may be accounted worthy to escape all these things that shall come to pass, and to stand before the Son of man.

John 12

35 Watch ye therefore: for ye know not when the master of the house cometh, at even, or at midnight, or at the cockcrowing, or in the morning:
36 Lest coming suddenly he find you sleeping.
37 And what I say unto you I say unto all, Watch.

Parable: The Ten Virgins

CHAPTER 25

1 Then shall the kingdom of heaven be likened unto ten virgins, which took their lamps, and went forth to meet the bridegroom.
2 And five of them were wise, and five were foolish.
3 They that were foolish took their lamps, and took no oil with them:
4 But the wise took oil in their vessels with their lamps.
5 While the bridegroom tarried, they all slumbered and slept.
6 And at midnight there was a cry made, Behold, the bridegroom cometh; go ye out to meet him.
7 Then all those virgins arose, and trimmed their lamps.
8 And the foolish said unto the wise, Give us of your oil; for our lamps are gone out.
9 But the wise answered, saying, Not so; lest there be not enough for us and you: but go ye rather to them that sell, and buy for yourselves.
10 And while they went to buy, the bridegroom came; and they that were ready went in with him to the marriage: and the door was shut.
11 Afterward came also the other virgins, saying, Lord, Lord, open to us.
12 But he answered and said, Verily I say unto you, I know you not.
13 Watch therefore, for ye know neither the day nor the hour wherein the Son of man cometh.

Parable: Talents

14 For the kingdom of heaven is as a man travelling into a far country, who called his own servants, and delivered unto them his goods.
15 And unto one he gave five talents, to another two, and to another one; to every man according to his several ability; and straightway took his journey.
16 Then he that had received the five talents went and traded with the same, and made them other five talents.
17 And likewise he that had received two, he also gained other two.
18 But he that had received one went and digged in the earth, and hid his lord's money.
19 After a long time the lord of those servants cometh, and reckoneth with them.
20 And so he that had received five talents came and brought other five talents, saying, Lord, thou deliveredst unto me five talents: behold, I have gained beside them five talents more.
21 His lord said unto him, Well done, thou good and faithful servant: thou hast been faithful over a few things, I will make thee ruler over many things: enter thou into the joy of thy lord.

Matthew 25

22 He also that had received two talents came and said,
Lord, thou deliveredst unto me two talents: behold, I have
gained two other talents beside them.
23 His lord said unto him, Well done, good and faithful
servant; thou hast been faithful over a few things, I will
make thee ruler over many things: enter thou into the joy
of thy lord.
24 Then he which had received the one talent came and
said, Lord, I knew thee that thou art an hard man, reaping
where thou hast not sown, and gathering where thou hast
not strawed:
25 And I was afraid, and went and hid thy talent in the
earth: lo, there thou hast that is thine.
26 His lord answered and said unto him, Thou wicked
and slothful servant, thou knewest that I reap where I
sowed not, and gather where I have not strawed:
27 Thou oughtest therefore to have put my money to the
exchangers, and then at my coming I should have received
mine own with usury.
28 Take therefore the talent from him, and give it unto
him which hath ten talents.
29 For unto every one that hath shall be given, and he
shall have abundance: but from him that hath not shall be
taken away even that which he hath.
30 And cast ye the unprofitable servant into outer dark-
ness: there shall be weeping and gnashing of teeth.

Mark 14

Luke 21

John 12

Parable: The Final Judgment

31 When the Son of man shall come in his glory, and all
the holy angels with him, then shall he sit upon the throne
of his glory:
32 And before him shall be gathered all nations: and he
shall separate them one from another, as a shepherd
divideth his sheep from the goats:
33 And he shall set the sheep on his right hand, but the
goats on the left.
34 Then shall the King say unto them on his right hand,
Come, ye blessed of my Father, inherit the kingdom pre-
pared for you from the foundation of the world:
35 For I was an hungred, and ye gave me meat: I was
thirsty, and ye gave me drink: I was a stranger, and ye took
me in:
36 Naked, and ye clothed me: I was sick, and ye visited
me: I was in prison, and ye came unto me.
37 Then shall the righteous answer him, saying, Lord,
when saw we thee an hungred, and fed thee? or thirsty, and
gave thee drink?
38 When saw we thee a stranger, and took thee in? or
naked, and clothed thee?
39 Or when saw we thee sick, or in prison, and came
unto thee?
40 And the King shall answer and say unto them, Verily
I say unto you, Inasmuch as ye have done it unto one of
the least of these my brethren, ye have done it unto me.
41 Then shall he say also unto them on the left hand,
Depart from me, ye cursed, into everlasting fire, prepared
for the devil and his angels:

42 For I was an hungred, and ye gave me no meat: I was thirsty, and ye gave me no drink:
43 I was a stranger, and ye took me not in: naked, and ye clothed me not: sick, and in prison, and ye visited me not.
44 Then shall they also answer him, saying, Lord, when saw we thee an hungred, or athirst, or a stranger, or naked, or sick, or in prison, and did not minister unto thee?
45 Then shall he answer them, saying, Verily I say unto you, Inasmuch as ye did it not to one of the least of these, ye did it not to me.
46 And these shall go away into everlasting punishment: but the righteous into life eternal.

CHAPTER 26

1 And it came to pass, when Jesus had finished all these sayings, he said unto his disciples,
2 Ye know that after two days is the feast of the passover, and the Son of man is betrayed to be crucified.
3 Then assembled together the chief priests, and the scribes, and the elders of the people, unto the palace of the high priest, who was called Caiaphas,
4 And consulted that they might take Jesus by subtilty, and kill him.
5 But they said, Not on the feast day, lest there be an uproar among the people.

CHAPTER 14

1 After two days was the feast of the passover, and of unleavened bread: and the chief priests and the scribes sought how they might take him by craft, and put him to death.

2 But they said, Not on the feast day, lest there be an uproar of the people.

37 And in the day time he was teaching in the temple; and at night he went out, and abode in the mount that is called the mount of Olives.
38 And all the people came early in the morning to him in the temple, for to hear him

CHAPTER 22

1 Now the feast of unleavened bread drew nigh, which is called the Passover.
2 And the chief priests and scribes sought how they might kill him; for they feared the people.

Christ Anointed with Oil

6 Now when Jesus was in Bethany, in the house of Simon the leper,
7 There came unto him a woman having an alabaster box of very precious ointment, and poured it on his head, as he sat at meat.
8 But when his disciples saw it, they had indignation, saying, To what purpose is this waste?

9 For this ointment might have been sold for much, and given to the poor.

10 When Jesus understood it, he said unto them, Why trouble ye the woman? for she hath wrought a good work upon me.
11 For ye have the poor always with you; but me ye have not always.
12 For in that she hath poured this ointment on my body, she did it for my burial.
13 Verily I say unto you, Wheresoever this gospel shall be preached in the whole world, there shall also this, that this woman hath done, be told for a memorial of her.

3 And being in Bethany in the house of Simon the leper, as he sat at meat, there came a woman having an alabaster box of ointment of spikenard very precious; and she brake the box, and poured it on his head.

4 And there were some that had indignation within themselves, and said, Why was this waste of the ointment made?
5 For it might have been sold for more than three hundred pence, and have been given to the poor. And they murmured against her.
6 And Jesus said, Let her alone; why trouble ye her? she hath wrought a good work on me.

7 For ye have the poor with you always, and whensoever ye will ye may do them good: but me ye have not always.
8 She hath done what she could: she is come aforehand to anoint my body to the burying.
9 Verily I say unto you, Wheresoever this gospel shall be preached throughout the whole world, this also that she hath done shall be spoken of for a memorial of her.

Judas Conspires to Betray Christ

14 Then one of the twelve, called Judas Iscariot, went unto the chief priests,

10 And Judas Iscariot, one of the twelve, went unto the chief priests, to betray him unto them.

3 Then entered Satan into Judas surnamed Iscariot, being of the number of the twelve.
4 And he went his way, and communed with the chief priests and captains, how he might betray him unto them.

Matthew 26	Mark 14	Luke 22	John 13
15 And said unto them, What will ye give me, and I will deliver him unto you? And they covenanted with him for thirty pieces of silver. 16 And from that time he sought opportunity to betray him.	11 And when they heard it, they were glad, and promised to give him money. And he sought how he might conveniently betray him.	5 And they were glad, and covenanted to give him money. 6 And he promised, and sought opportunity to betray him unto them in the absence of the multitude.	

Reading for Day 5

The Last Supper

Matthew 26	Mark 14	Luke 22	John 13
			CHAPTER 13 1 Now before the feast of the passover, when Jesus knew that his hour was come that he should depart out of this world unto the Father, having loved his own which were in the world, he loved them unto the end.
17 Now the first day of the feast of unleavened bread the disciples came to Jesus, saying unto him, Where wilt thou that we prepare for thee to eat the passover?	12 And the first day of unleavened bread, when they killed the passover, his disciples said unto him, Where wilt thou that we go and prepare that thou mayest eat the passover?	7 Then came the day of unleavened bread, when the passover must be killed.	
		8 And he sent Peter and John, saying, Go and prepare us the passover, that we may eat. 9 And they said unto him, Where wilt thou that we prepare?	
18 And he said, Go into the city to such a man, and say unto him, The Master saith, My time is at hand; I will keep the passover at thy house with my disciples.	13 And he sendeth forth two of his disciples, and saith unto them, Go ye into the city, and there shall meet you a man bearing a pitcher of water: follow him. 14 And wheresoever he shall go in, say ye to the goodman of the house, The Master saith, Where is the guestchamber, where I shall eat the passover with my disciples?	10 And he said unto them, Behold, when ye are entered into the city, there shall a man meet you, bearing a pitcher of water; follow him into the house where he entereth in. 11 And ye shall say unto the goodman of the house, The Master saith unto thee, Where is the guestchamber, where I shall eat the passover with my disciples?	
	15 And he will shew you a large upper room furnished and prepared: there make ready for us.	12 And he shall shew you a large upper room furnished: there make ready.	
19 And the disciples did as Jesus had appointed them; and they made ready the passover.	16 And his disciples went forth, and came into the city, and found as he had said unto them: and they made ready the passover.	13 And they went, and found as he had said unto them: and they made ready the passover.	
20 Now when the even was come, he sat down with the twelve.	17 And in the evening he cometh with the twelve.	14 And when the hour was come, he sat down, and the twelve apostles with him. 15 And he said unto them, With desire I have desired to eat this passover with you before I suffer: 16 For I say unto you, I will not any more eat thereof, until it be fulfilled in the kingdom of God. 17 And he took the cup, and gave thanks, and said, Take this, and divide it among yourselves:	
29 But I say unto you, I will not drink henceforth of this fruit of the vine, until that day when I drink it new with you in my Father's kingdom.	**25** Verily I say unto you, I will drink no more of the fruit of the vine, until that day that I drink it new in the kingdom of God.	18 For I say unto you, I will not drink of the fruit of the vine, until the kingdom of God shall come.	
			2 And supper being ended, the devil having now put into the heart of Judas Iscariot, Simon's son, to betray him; **18** I speak not of you all: I know whom I have chosen: but that the scripture may be fulfilled, He that eateth bread with me hath lifted up his heel against me. **19** Now I tell you before it come, that, when it is come to pass, ye may believe that I am he. **20** Verily, verily, I say unto you, He that receiveth whomsoever I send receiveth me; and he that receiveth me receiveth him that sent me.

21 And as they did eat, he said, Verily I say unto you, that one of you shall betray me.	18 And as they sat and did eat, Jesus said, Verily I say unto you, One of you which eateth with me shall betray me.	**21** But, behold, the hand of him that betrayeth me is with me on the table.	**21** When Jesus had thus said, he was troubled in spirit, and testified, and said, Verily, verily, I say unto you, that one of you shall betray me. **22** Then the disciples looked one on another, doubting of whom he spake.
22 And they were exceeding sorrowful, and began every one of them to say unto him, Lord, is it I? 23 And he answered and said, He that dippeth his hand with me in the dish, the same shall betray me. 24 The Son of man goeth as it is written of him: but woe unto that man by whom the Son of man is betrayed! it had been good for that man if he had not been born.	19 And they began to be sorrowful, and to say unto him one by one, Is it I? and another said, Is it I? 20 And he answered and said unto them, It is one of the twelve, that dippeth with me in the dish. 21 The Son of man indeed goeth, as it is written of him: but woe to that man by whom the Son of man is betrayed! good were it for that man if he had never been born.	**23** And they began to enquire among themselves, which of them it was that should do this thing. **22** And truly the Son of man goeth, as it was determined: but woe unto that man by whom he is betrayed!	**23** Now there was leaning on Jesus' bosom one of his disciples, whom Jesus loved. **24** Simon Peter therefore beckoned to him, that he should ask who it should be of whom he spake. **25** He then lying on Jesus' breast saith unto him, Lord, who is it? **26** Jesus answered, He it is, to whom I shall give a sop, when I have dipped it. And when he had dipped the sop, he gave it to Judas Iscariot, the son of Simon.
25 Then Judas, which betrayed him, answered and said, Master, is it I? He said unto him, Thou hast said.			**27** And after the sop Satan entered into him. Then said Jesus unto him, That thou doest, do quickly. **28** Now no man at the table knew for what intent he spake this unto him. **29** For some of them thought, because Judas had the bag, that Jesus had said unto him, Buy those things that we have need of against the feast; or, that he should give something to the poor. **30** He then having received the sop went immediately out: and it was night.
		24 And there was also a strife among them, which of them should be accounted the greatest. **25** And he said unto them, The kings of the Gentiles exercise lordship over them; and they that exercise authority upon them are called benefactors. **26** But ye shall not be so: but he that is greatest among you, let him be as the younger; and he that is chief, as he that doth serve. **27** For whether is greater, he that sitteth at meat, or he that serveth? is not he that sitteth at meat? but I am among you as he that serveth. **28** Ye are they which have continued with me in my temptations. **29** And I appoint unto you a kingdom, as my Father hath appointed unto me; **30** That ye may eat and drink at my table in my kingdom, and sit on thrones judging the twelve tribes of Israel.	

Institution of the Sacrament

26 And as they were eating, Jesus took bread, and blessed it, and brake it, and gave it to the disciples, and said, Take, eat; this is my body. 27 And he took the cup, and gave thanks, and gave it to them, saying, Drink ye all of it; 28 For this is my blood of the new testament, which is shed for many for the remission of sins.	22 And as they did eat, Jesus took bread, and blessed, and brake it, and gave to them, and said, Take, eat: this is my body. 23 And he took the cup, and when he had given thanks, he gave it to them: and they all drank of it. 24 And he said unto them, This is my blood of the new testament, which is shed for many.	19 And he took bread, and gave thanks, and brake it, and gave unto them, saying, This is my body which is given for you: this do in remembrance of me. 20 Likewise also the cup after supper, saying, This cup is the new testament in my blood, which is shed for you.	

Matthew 26	Mark 14	Luke 22	John 13
29 But I say unto you, I will not drink henceforth of this fruit of the vine, until that day when I drink it new with you in my Father's kingdom.	25 Verily I say unto you, I will drink no more of the fruit of the vine, until that day that I drink it new in the kingdom of God.	**15** And he said unto them, With desire I have desired to eat this passover with you before I suffer: **16** For I say unto you, I will not any more eat thereof, until it be fulfilled in the kingdom of God. **17** And he took the cup, and gave thanks, and said, Take this, and divide it among yourselves: **18** For I say unto you, I will not drink of the fruit of the vine, until the kingdom of God shall come.	

Washing of the Apostles' Feet

Matthew 26	Mark 14	Luke 22	John 13
			3 Jesus knowing that the Father had given all things into his hands, and that he was come from God, and went to God; 4 He riseth from supper, and laid aside his garments; and took a towel, and girded himself. 5 After that he poureth water into a bason, and began to wash the disciples' feet, and to wipe them with the towel wherewith he was girded. 6 Then cometh he to Simon Peter: and Peter saith unto him, Lord, dost thou wash my feet? 7 Jesus answered and said unto him, What I do thou knowest not now; but thou shalt know hereafter. 8 Peter saith unto him, Thou shalt never wash my feet. Jesus answered him, If I wash thee not, thou hast no part with me. 9 Simon Peter saith unto him, Lord, not my feet only, but also my hands and my head. 10 Jesus saith to him, He that is washed needeth not save to wash his feet, but is clean every whit: and ye are clean, but not all. 11 For he knew who should betray him; therefore said he, Ye are not all clean. 12 So after he had washed their feet, and had taken his garments, and was set down again, he said unto them, Know ye what I have done to you? 13 Ye call me Master and Lord: and ye say well; for so I am. 14 If I then, your Lord and Master, have washed your feet; ye also ought to wash one another's feet. 15 For I have given you an example, that ye should do as I have done to you. 16 Verily, verily, I say unto you, The servant is not greater than his lord; neither he that is sent greater than he that sent him. 17 If ye know these things, happy are ye if ye do them. 18 I speak not of you all: I know whom I have chosen: but that the scripture may be fulfilled, He that eateth bread with me hath lifted up his heel against me. 19 Now I tell you before it come, that, when it is come to pass, ye may believe that I am he. 20 Verily, verily, I say unto you, He that receiveth whomsoever I send receiveth me; and he that receiveth me receiveth him that sent me. **31** Therefore, when he was gone out, Jesus said, Now is the Son of man glorified, and God is glorified in him.

32 If God be glorified in him, God shall also glorify him in himself, and shall straightway glorify him.

33 Little children, yet a little while I am with you. Ye shall seek me: and as I said unto the Jews, Whither I go, ye cannot come; so now I say to you.

34 A new commandment I give unto you, That ye love one another; as I have loved you, that ye also love one another.

35 By this shall all men know that ye are my disciples, if ye have love one to another.

36 Simon Peter said unto him, Lord, whither goest thou? Jesus answered him, Whither I go, thou canst not follow me now; but thou shalt follow me afterwards.

37 Peter said unto him, Lord, why cannot I follow thee now? I will lay down my life for thy sake.

38 Jesus answered him, Wilt thou lay down thy life for my sake? Verily, verily, I say unto thee, The cock shall not crow, till thou hast denied me thrice.

Discourse on the Second Comforter

CHAPTER 14

1 Let not your heart be troubled: ye believe in God, believe also in me.

2 In my Father's house are many mansions: if it were not so, I would have told you. I go to prepare a place for you.

3 And if I go and prepare a place for you, I will come again, and receive you unto myself; that where I am, there ye may be also.

4 And whither I go ye know, and the way ye know.

5 Thomas saith unto him, Lord, we know not whither thou goest; and how can we know the way?

6 Jesus saith unto him, I am the way, the truth, and the life: no man cometh unto the Father, but by me.

7 If ye had known me, ye should have known my Father also: and from henceforth ye know him, and have seen him.

8 Philip saith unto him, Lord, shew us the Father, and it sufficeth us.

9 Jesus saith unto him, Have I been so long time with you, and yet hast thou not known me, Philip? he that hath seen me hath seen the Father; and how sayest thou then, Shew us the Father?

10 Believest thou not that I am in the Father, and the Father in me? the words that I speak unto you I speak not of myself: but the Father that dwelleth in me, he doeth the works.

11 Believe me that I am in the Father, and the Father in me: or else believe me for the very works' sake.

12 Verily, verily, I say unto you, He that believeth on me, the works that I do shall he do also; and greater works than these shall he do; because I go unto my Father.

13 And whatsoever ye shall ask in my name, that will I do, that the Father may be glorified in the Son.

14 If ye shall ask any thing in my name, I will do it.

15 If ye love me, keep my commandments.

16 And I will pray the Father, and he shall give you another Comforter, that he may abide with you for ever;

17 Even the Spirit of truth; whom the world cannot receive, because it seeth him not, neither knoweth him: but ye know him; for he dwelleth with you, and shall be in you.

18 I will not leave you comfortless: I will come to you.
19 Yet a little while, and the world seeth me no more;
but ye see me: because I live, ye shall live also.
20 At that day ye shall know that I am in my Father, and
ye in me, and I in you.
21 He that hath my commandments, and keepeth them,
he it is that loveth me: and he that loveth me shall be
loved of my Father, and I will love him, and will manifest
myself to him.
22 Judas saith unto him, not Iscariot, Lord, how is it that
thou wilt manifest thyself unto us, and not unto the world?
23 Jesus answered and said unto him, If a man love me,
he will keep my words: and my Father will love him, and
we will come unto him, and make our abode with him.
24 He that loveth me not keepeth not my sayings: and
the word which ye hear is not mine, but the Father's which
sent me.
25 These things have I spoken unto you, being yet pre-
sent with you.
26 But the Comforter, which is the Holy Ghost, whom
the Father will send in my name, he shall teach you all
things, and bring all things to your remembrance, whatso-
ever I have said unto you.
27 Peace I leave with you, my peace I give unto you: not
as the world giveth, give I unto you. Let not your heart be
troubled, neither let it be afraid.
28 Ye have heard how I said unto you, I go away, and
come again unto you. If ye loved me, ye would rejoice,
because I said, I go unto the Father: for my Father is greater
than I.
29 And now I have told you before it come to pass, that,
when it is come to pass, ye might believe.
30 Hereafter I will not talk much with you: for the
prince of this world cometh, and hath nothing in me.
31 But that the world may know that I love the Father;
and as the Father gave me commandment, even so I do.
Arise, let us go hence.

CHRIST TEACHES THE APOSTLES

CHAPTER 15

1 I am the true vine, and my Father is the husbandman.
2 Every branch in me that beareth not fruit he taketh
away: and every branch that beareth fruit, he purgeth it,
that it may bring forth more fruit.
3 Now ye are clean through the word which I have spo-
ken unto you.
4 Abide in me, and I in you. As the branch cannot bear
fruit of itself, except it abide in the vine; no more can ye,
except ye abide in me.
5 I am the vine, ye are the branches: He that abideth in
me, and I in him, the same bringeth forth much fruit: for
without me ye can do nothing.
6 If a man abide not in me, he is cast forth as a branch,
and is withered; and men gather them, and cast them into
the fire, and they are burned.
7 If ye abide in me, and my words abide in you, ye shall
ask what ye will, and it shall be done unto you.

8 Herein is my Father glorified, that ye bear much fruit;
so shall ye be my disciples.
9 As the Father hath loved me, so have I loved you: con-
tinue ye in my love.
10 If ye keep my commandments, ye shall abide in my
love; even as I have kept my Father's commandments, and
abide in his love.
11 These things have I spoken unto you, that my joy
might remain in you, and that your joy might be full.
12 This is my commandment, That ye love one another,
as I have loved you.
13 Greater love hath no man than this, that a man lay
down his life for his friends.
14 Ye are my friends, if ye do whatsoever I command you.
15 Henceforth I call you not servants; for the servant
knoweth not what his lord doeth: but I have called you
friends; for all things that I have heard of my Father I have
made known unto you.
16 Ye have not chosen me, but I have chosen you, and
ordained you, that ye should go and bring forth fruit, and
that your fruit should remain: that whatsoever ye shall ask
of the Father in my name, he may give it you.
17 These things I command you, that ye love one another.
18 If the world hate you, ye know that it hated me before
it hated you.
19 If ye were of the world, the world would love his own:
but because ye are not of the world, but I have chosen you
out of the world, therefore the world hateth you.
20 Remember the word that I said unto you, The servant
is not greater than his lord. If they have persecuted me,
they will also persecute you; if they have kept my saying,
they will keep yours also.
21 But all these things will they do unto you for my
name's sake, because they know not him that sent me.
22 If I had not come and spoken unto them, they had
not had sin: but now they have no cloke for their sin.
23 He that hateth me hateth my Father also.
24 If I had not done among them the works which none
other man did, they had not had sin: but now have they
both seen and hated both me and my Father.
25 But this cometh to pass, that the word might be ful-
filled that is written in their law, They hated me without a
cause.
26 But when the Comforter is come, whom I will send
unto you from the Father, even the Spirit of truth, which
proceedeth from the Father, he shall testify of me:
27 And ye also shall bear witness, because ye have been
with me from the beginning.

CHAPTER 16

1 These things have I spoken unto you, that ye should
not be offended.
2 They shall put you out of the synagogues: yea, the time
cometh, that whosoever killeth you will think that he
doeth God service.
3 And these things will they do unto you, because they
have not known the Father, nor me.
4 But these things have I told you, that when the time
shall come, ye may remember that I told you of them. And
these things I said not unto you at the beginning, because
I was with you.

Matthew 26

Mark 14

Luke 22

John 16

5 But now I go my way to him that sent me; and none of
you asketh me, Whither goest thou?
6 But because I have said these things unto you, sorrow
hath filled your heart.
7 Nevertheless I tell you the truth; It is expedient for you
that I go away: for if I go not away, the Comforter will not
come unto you; but if I depart, I will send him unto you.
8 And when he is come, he will reprove the world of sin,
and of righteousness, and of judgment:
9 Of sin, because they believe not on me;
10 Of righteousness, because I go to my Father, and ye
see me no more;
11 Of judgment, because the prince of this world is
judged.
12 I have yet many things to say unto you, but ye cannot
bear them now.
13 Howbeit when he, the Spirit of truth, is come, he will
guide you into all truth: for he shall not speak of himself;
but whatsoever he shall hear, that shall he speak: and he
will shew you things to come.
14 He shall glorify me: for he shall receive of mine, and
shall shew it unto you.
15 All things that the Father hath are mine: therefore said
I, that he shall take of mine, and shall shew it unto you.
16 A little while, and ye shall not see me: and again, a
little while, and ye shall see me, because I go to the Father.
17 Then said some of his disciples among themselves,
What is this that he saith unto us, A little while, and ye
shall not see me: and again, a little while, and ye shall see
me: and, Because I go to the Father?
18 They said therefore, What is this that he saith, A
little while? we cannot tell what he saith.
19 Now Jesus knew that they were desirous to ask him,
and said unto them, Do ye enquire among yourselves of
that I said, A little while, and ye shall not see me: and
again, a little while, and ye shall see me?
20 Verily, verily, I say unto you, That ye shall weep and
lament, but the world shall rejoice: and ye shall be sorrow-
ful, but your sorrow shall be turned into joy.
21 A woman when she is in travail hath sorrow, because
her hour is come: but as soon as she is delivered of the
child, she remembereth no more the anguish, for joy that a
man is born into the world.
22 And ye now therefore have sorrow: but I will see you
again, and your heart shall rejoice, and your joy no man
taketh from you.
23 And in that day ye shall ask me nothing. Verily, ver-
ily, I say unto you, Whatsoever ye shall ask the Father in
my name, he will give it you.
24 Hitherto have ye asked nothing in my name: ask, and
ye shall receive, that your joy may be full.
25 These things have I spoken unto you in proverbs: but
the time cometh, when I shall no more speak unto you in
proverbs, but I shall shew you plainly of the Father.
26 At that day ye shall ask in my name: and I say not
unto you, that I will pray the Father for you:
27 For the Father himself loveth you, because ye have
loved me, and have believed that I came out from God.

31 Then saith Jesus unto them, All ye shall be offended because of me this night: for it is written, I will smite the shepherd, and the sheep of the flock shall be scattered abroad. **32** But after I am risen again, I will go before you into Galilee.	**27** And Jesus saith unto them, All ye shall be offended because of me this night: for it is written, I will smite the shepherd, and the sheep shall be scattered. **28** But after that I am risen, I will go before you into Galilee.		28 I came forth from the Father, and am come into the world: again, I leave the world, and go to the Father. 29 His disciples said unto him, Lo, now speakest thou plainly, and speakest no proverb. 30 Now are we sure that thou knowest all things, and needest not that any man should ask thee: by this we believe that thou camest forth from God. 31 Jesus answered them, Do ye now believe? 32 Behold, the hour cometh, yea, is now come, that ye shall be scattered, every man to his own, and shall leave me alone: and yet I am not alone, because the Father is with me. 33 These things I have spoken unto you, that in me ye might have peace. In the world ye shall have tribulation: but be of good cheer; I have overcome the world.

Intercessory Prayer

			CHAPTER 17 1 These words spake Jesus, and lifted up his eyes to heaven, and said, Father, the hour is come; glorify thy Son, that thy Son also may glorify thee: 2 As thou hast given him power over all flesh, that he should give eternal life to as many as thou hast given him. 3 And this is life eternal, that they might know thee the only true God, and Jesus Christ, whom thou hast sent. 4 I have glorified thee on the earth: I have finished the work which thou gavest me to do. 5 And now, O Father, glorify thou me with thine own self with the glory which I had with thee before the world was. 6 I have manifested thy name unto the men which thou gavest me out of the world: thine they were, and thou gavest them me; and they have kept thy word. 7 Now they have known that all things whatsoever thou hast given me are of thee. 8 For I have given unto them the words which thou gavest me; and they have received them, and have known surely that I came out from thee, and they have believed that thou didst send me. 9 I pray for them: I pray not for the world, but for them which thou hast given me; for they are thine. 10 And all mine are thine, and thine are mine; and I am glorified in them. 11 And now I am no more in the world, but these are in the world, and I come to thee. Holy Father, keep through thine own name those whom thou hast given me, that they may be one, as we are. 12 While I was with them in the world, I kept them in thy name: those that thou gavest me I have kept, and none of them is lost, but the son of perdition; that the scripture might be fulfilled. 13 And now come I to thee; and these things I speak in the world, that they might have my joy fulfilled in themselves. 14 I have given them thy word; and the world hath hated them, because they are not of the world, even as I am not of the world.

Matthew 26

Mark 14

Luke 22

John 17

15 I pray not that thou shouldest take them out of the world, but that thou shouldest keep them from the evil.
16 They are not of the world, even as I am not of the world.
17 Sanctify them through thy truth: thy word is truth.
18 As thou hast sent me into the world, even so have I also sent them into the world.
19 And for their sakes I sanctify myself, that they also might be sanctified through the truth.
20 Neither pray I for these alone, but for them also which shall believe on me through their word;
21 That they all may be one; as thou, Father, art in me, and I in thee, that they also may be one in us: that the world may believe that thou hast sent me.
22 And the glory which thou gavest me I have given them; that they may be one, even as we are one:
23 I in them, and thou in me, that they may be made perfect in one; and that the world may know that thou hast sent me, and hast loved them, as thou hast loved me.
24 Father, I will that they also, whom thou hast given me, be with me where I am; that they may behold my glory, which thou hast given me: for thou lovedst me before the foundation of the world.
25 O righteous Father, the world hath not known thee: but I have known thee, and these have known that thou hast sent me.
26 And I have declared unto them thy name, and will declare it: that the love wherewith thou hast loved me may be in them, and I in them.

Prayer in Gethsemane

Matthew 26

30 And when they had sung an hymn, they went out into the mount of Olives.

33 Peter answered and said unto him, Though all men shall be offended because of thee, yet will I never be offended.

34 Jesus said unto him, Verily I say unto thee, That this night, before the cock crow, thou shalt deny me thrice.

35 Peter said unto him, Though I should die with thee, yet will I not deny thee. Likewise also said all the disciples.

Mark 14

26 And when they had sung an hymn, they went out into the mount of Olives.

29 But Peter said unto him, Although all shall be offended, yet will not I.

30 And Jesus saith unto him, Verily I say unto thee, That this day, even in this night, before the cock crow twice, thou shalt deny me thrice.
31 But he spake the more vehemently, If I should die with thee, I will not deny thee in any wise. Likewise also said they all.

Luke 22

39 And he came and went out, as he was wont, to the Mount of Olives; and his disciples also followed him

31 And the Lord said, Simon, Simon, behold, Satan hath desired to have you, that he may sift you as wheat:
32 But I have prayed for thee, that thy faith fail not; and when thou art converted, strengthen thy brethren.

33 And he said unto him, Lord, I am ready to go with thee, both into prison, and to death.
34 And he said, I tell thee, Peter, the cock shall not crow this day, before thou shalt thrice deny that thou knowest me.

John

CHAPTER 18

1 When Jesus had spoken these words, he went forth with his disciples over the brook Cedron, where was a garden, into the which he entered, and his disciples.

(FROM CHAPTER 13)

36 Simon Peter said unto him, Lord, whither goest thou? Jesus answered him, Whither I go, thou canst not follow me now; but thou shalt follow me afterwards.
37 Peter said unto him, Lord, why cannot I follow thee now? I will lay down my life for thy sake.
38 Jesus answered him, Wilt thou lay down thy life for my sake? Verily, verily, I say unto thee, The cock shall not crow, till thou hast denied me thrice

36 Then cometh Jesus with them unto a place called Gethsemane, and saith unto the disciples, Sit ye here, while I go and pray yonder.
37 And he took with him Peter and the two sons of Zebedee, and began to be sorrowful and very heavy.
38 Then saith he unto them, My soul is exceeding sorrowful, even unto death: tarry ye here, and watch with me.
39 And he went a little further, and fell on his face, and prayed, saying, O my Father, if it be possible, let this cup pass from me: nevertheless not as I will, but as thou wilt.

40 And he cometh unto the disciples, and findeth them asleep, and saith unto Peter, What, could ye not watch with me one hour?
41 Watch and pray, that ye enter not into temptation: the spirit indeed is willing, but the flesh is weak.
42 He went away again the second time, and prayed, saying, O my Father, if this cup may not pass away from me, except I drink it, thy will be done.
43 And he came and found them asleep again: for their eyes were heavy.

44 And he left them, and went away again, and prayed the third time, saying the same words.
45 Then cometh he to his disciples, and saith unto them, Sleep on now, and take your rest: behold, the hour is at hand, and the Son of man is betrayed into the hands of sinners.

32 And they came to a place which was named Gethsemane: and he saith to his disciples, Sit ye here, while I shall pray.
33 And he taketh with him Peter and James and John, and began to be sore amazed, and to be very heavy;
34 And saith unto them, My soul is exceeding sorrowful unto death: tarry ye here, and watch.
35 And he went forward a little, and fell on the ground, and prayed that, if it were possible, the hour might pass from him.
36 And he said, Abba, Father, all things are possible unto thee; take away this cup from me: nevertheless not what I will, but what thou wilt.

37 And he cometh, and findeth them sleeping, and saith unto Peter, Simon, sleepest thou? couldest not thou watch one hour?
38 Watch ye and pray, lest ye enter into temptation. The spirit truly is ready, but the flesh is weak.
39 And again he went away, and prayed, and spake the same words.

40 And when he returned, he found them asleep again, (for their eyes were heavy,) neither wist they what to answer him.

41 And he cometh the third time, and saith unto them, Sleep on now, and take your rest: it is enough, the hour is come; behold, the Son of man is betrayed into the hands of sinners.

35 And he said unto them, When I sent you without purse, and scrip, and shoes, lacked ye any thing? And they said, Nothing.
36 Then said he unto them, But now, he that hath a purse, let him take it, and likewise his scrip: and he that hath no sword, let him sell his garment, and buy one.
37 For I say unto you, that this that is written must yet be accomplished in me, And he was reckoned among the transgressors: for the things concerning me have an end.
38 And they said, Lord, behold, here are two swords. And he said unto them, It is enough.

40 And when he was at the place, he said unto them, Pray that ye enter not into temptation.
41 And he was withdrawn from them about a stone's cast, and kneeled down, and prayed,
42 Saying, Father, if thou be willing, remove this cup from me: nevertheless not my will, but thine, be done.
43 And there appeared an angel unto him from heaven, strengthening him.
44 And being in an agony he prayed more earnestly: and his sweat was as it were great drops of blood falling down to the ground.
45 And when he rose up from prayer, and was come to his disciples, he found them sleeping for sorrow,
46 And said unto them, Why sleep ye? rise and pray, lest ye enter into temptation.

Betrayal

46 Rise, let us be going: behold, he is at hand that doth betray me.
47 And while he yet spake, lo, Judas, one of the twelve, came, and with him a great multitude with swords and staves, from the chief priests and elders of the people.

48 Now he that betrayed him gave them a sign, saying, Whomsoever I shall kiss, that same is he: hold him fast.

42 Rise up, let us go; lo, he that betrayeth me is at hand.

43 And immediately, while he yet spake, cometh Judas, one of the twelve, and with him a great multitude with swords and staves, from the chief priests and the scribes and the elders.
44 And he that betrayed him had given them a token, saying, Whomsoever I shall kiss, that same is he; take him, and lead him away safely.

47 And while he yet spake, behold a multitude, and he that was called Judas, one of the twelve, went before them, and drew near unto Jesus to kiss him.

CHAPTER 18

2 And Judas also, which betrayed him, knew the place: for Jesus ofttimes resorted thither with his disciples.
3 Judas then, having received a band of men and officers from the chief priests and Pharisees, cometh thither with lanterns and torches and weapons.

MATTHEW 26	MARK 14	LUKE 22	JOHN 18
49 And forthwith he came to Jesus, and said, Hail, master; and kissed him.	45 And as soon as he was come, he goeth straightway to him, and saith, Master, master; and kissed him.	48 But Jesus said unto him, Judas, betrayest thou the Son of man with a kiss?	
50 And Jesus said unto him, Friend, wherefore art thou come? Then came they, and laid hands on Jesus, and took him.	46 And they laid their hands on him, and took him.		4 Jesus therefore, knowing all things that should come upon him, went forth, and said unto them, Whom seek ye? 5 They answered him, Jesus of Nazareth. Jesus saith unto them, I am he. And Judas also, which betrayed him, stood with them. 6 As soon then as he had said unto them, I am he, they went backward, and fell to the ground. 7 Then asked he them again, Whom seek ye? And they said, Jesus of Nazareth. 8 Jesus answered, I have told you that I am he: if therefore ye seek me, let these go their way: 9 That the saying might be fulfilled, which he spake, Of them which thou gavest me have I lost none.
51 And, behold, one of them which were with Jesus stretched out his hand, and drew his sword, and struck a servant of the high priest's, and smote off his ear. 52 Then said Jesus unto him, Put up again thy sword into his place: for all they that take the sword shall perish with the sword. 53 Thinkest thou that I cannot now pray to my Father, and he shall presently give me more than twelve legions of angels? 54 But how then shall the scriptures be fulfilled, that thus it must be?	47 And one of them that stood by drew a sword, and smote a servant of the high priest, and cut off his ear.	49 When they which were about him saw what would follow, they said unto him, Lord, shall we smite with the sword? 50 And one of them smote the servant of the high priest, and cut off his right ear. 51 And Jesus answered and said, Suffer ye thus far. And he touched his ear, and healed him.	10 Then Simon Peter having a sword drew it, and smote the high priest's servant, and cut off his right ear. The servant's name was Malchus. 11 Then said Jesus unto Peter, Put up thy sword into the sheath: the cup which my Father hath given me, shall I not drink it?
55 In that same hour said Jesus to the multitudes, Are ye come out as against a thief with swords and staves for to take me? I sat daily with you teaching in the temple, and ye laid no hold on me. 56 But all this was done, that the scriptures of the prophets might be fulfilled. Then all the disciples forsook him, and fled.	48 And Jesus answered and said unto them, Are ye come out, as against a thief, with swords and with staves to take me? 49 I was daily with you in the temple teaching, and ye took me not: but the scriptures must be fulfilled. 50 And they all forsook him, and fled. 51 And there followed him a certain young man, having a linen cloth cast about his naked body; and the young men laid hold on him: 52 And he left the linen cloth, and fled from them naked.	52 Then Jesus said unto the chief priests, and captains of the temple, and the elders, which were come to him, Be ye come out, as against a thief, with swords and staves? 53 When I was daily with you in the temple, ye stretched forth no hands against me: but this is your hour, and the power of darkness.	
			12 Then the band and the captain and officers of the Jews took Jesus, and bound him,

CHRIST BEFORE CAIAPHAS AND THE COUNCIL

MATTHEW 26	MARK 14	LUKE 22	JOHN 18
57 And they that had laid hold on Jesus led him away to Caiaphas the high priest, where the scribes and the elders were assembled.	53 And they led Jesus away to the high priest: and with him were assembled all the chief priests and the elders and the scribes.	54 Then took they him, and led him, and brought him into the high priest's house. And Peter followed afar off.	13 And led him away to Annas first; for he was father in law to Caiaphas, which was the high priest that same year. 14 Now Caiaphas was he, which gave counsel to the

58 But Peter followed him afar off unto the high priest's palace, and went in, and sat with the servants, to see the end.

59 Now the chief priests, and elders, and all the council, sought false witness against Jesus, to put him to death;
60 But found none: yea, though many false witnesses came, yet found they none. At the last came two false witnesses,

61 And said, This fellow said, I am able to destroy the temple of God, and to build it in three days.

62 And the high priest arose, and said unto him, Answerest thou nothing? what is it which these witness against thee?
63 But Jesus held his peace. And the high priest answered and said unto him, I adjure thee by the living God, that thou tell us whether thou be the Christ, the Son of God.

64 Jesus saith unto him, Thou hast said: nevertheless I say unto you, Hereafter shall ye see the Son of man sitting on the right hand of power, and coming in the clouds of heaven.
65 Then the high priest rent his clothes, saying, He hath spoken blasphemy; what further need have we of witnesses? behold, now ye have heard his blasphemy.
66 What think ye? They answered and said, He is guilty of death.
67 Then did they spit in his face, and buffeted him; and others smote him with the palms of their hands,
68 Saying, Prophesy unto us, thou Christ, Who is he that smote thee?

54 And Peter followed him afar off, even into the palace of the high priest: and he sat with the servants, and warmed himself at the fire.

55 And the chief priests and all the council sought for witness against Jesus to put him to death; and found none.
56 For many bare false witness against him, but their witness agreed not together.
57 And there arose certain, and bare false witness against him, saying,
58 We heard him say, I will destroy this temple that is made with hands, and within three days I will build another made without hands.
59 But neither so did their witness agree together.
60 And the high priest stood up in the midst, and asked Jesus, saying, Answerest thou nothing? what is it which these witness against thee?
61 But he held his peace, and answered nothing. Again the high priest asked him, and said unto him, Art thou the Christ, the Son of the Blessed?

62 And Jesus said, I am: and ye shall see the Son of man sitting on the right hand of power, and coming in the clouds of heaven.

63 Then the high priest rent his clothes, and saith, What need we any further witnesses?
64 Ye have heard the blasphemy: what think ye? And they all condemned him to be guilty of death.

65 And some began to spit on him, and to cover his face, and to buffet him, and to say unto him, Prophesy: and the servants did strike him with the palms of their hands.

66 And as soon as it was day, the elders of the people and the chief priests and the scribes came together, and led him into their council, saying,
67 Art thou the Christ? tell us. And he said unto them, If I tell you, ye will not believe:

68 And if I also ask you, ye will not answer me, nor let me go.
69 Hereafter shall the Son of man sit on the right hand of the power of God.
70 Then said they all, Art thou then the Son of God? And he said unto them, Ye say that I am.
71 And they said, What need we any further witness? for we ourselves have heard of his own mouth.

Jews, that it was expedient that one man should die for the people.
15 And Simon Peter followed Jesus, and so did another disciple: that disciple was known unto the high priest, and went in with Jesus into the palace of the high priest.
16 But Peter stood at the door without. Then went out that other disciple, which was known unto the high priest, and spake unto her that kept the door, and brought in Peter.
17 Then saith the damsel that kept the door unto Peter, Art not thou also one of this man's disciples? He saith, I am not.
18 And the servants and officers stood there, who had made a fire of coals; for it was cold: and they warmed themselves: and Peter stood with them, and warmed himself.
19 The high priest then asked Jesus of his disciples, and of his doctrine.
20 Jesus answered him, I spake openly to the world; I ever taught in the synagogue, and in the temple, whither the Jews always resort; and in secret have I said nothing.
21 Why askest thou me? ask them which heard me, what I have said unto them: behold, they know what I said.
22 And when he had thus spoken, one of the officers which stood by struck Jesus with the palm of his hand, saying, Answerest thou the high priest so?
23 Jesus answered him, If I have spoken evil, bear witness of the evil: but if well, why smitest thou me?
24 Now Annas had sent him bound unto Caiaphas the high priest.

Peter's Denial

Matthew 26	Mark 14	Luke 22	John 18
69 Now Peter sat without in the palace: and a damsel came unto him, saying, Thou also wast with Jesus of Galilee.	66 And as Peter was beneath in the palace, there cometh one of the maids of the high priest: 67 And when she saw Peter warming himself, she looked upon him, and said, And thou also wast with Jesus of Nazareth.	55 And when they had kindled a fire in the midst of the hall, and were set down together, Peter sat down among them. 56 But a certain maid beheld him as he sat by the fire, and earnestly looked upon him, and said, This man was also with him.	**17** Then saith the damsel that kept the door unto Peter, Art not thou also one of this man's disciples? He saith, I am not. **18** And the servants and officers stood there, who had made a fire of coals; for it was cold: and they warmed themselves: and Peter stood with them, and warmed himself.
70 But he denied before them all, saying, I know not what thou sayest.	68 But he denied, saying, I know not, neither understand I what thou sayest. And he went out into the porch; and the cock crew.	57 And he denied him, saying, Woman, I know him not.	
71 And when he was gone out into the porch, another maid saw him, and said unto them that were there, This fellow was also with Jesus of Nazareth.	69 And a maid saw him again, and began to say to them that stood by, This is one of them.	58 And after a little while another saw him, and said, Thou art also of them. And Peter said, Man, I am not.	**25** And Simon Peter stood and warmed himself. They said therefore unto him, Art not thou also one of his disciples? He denied it, and said, I am not.
72 And again he denied with an oath, I do not know the man. 73 And after a while came unto him they that stood by, and said to Peter, Surely thou also art one of them; for thy speech bewrayeth thee. 74 Then began he to curse and to swear, saying, I know not the man. And immediately the cock crew. 75 And Peter remembered the word of Jesus, which said unto him, Before the cock crow, thou shalt deny me thrice. And he went out, and wept bitterly.	70 And he denied it again. And a little after, they that stood by said again to Peter, Surely thou art one of them: for thou art a Galilaean, and thy speech agreeth thereto. 71 But he began to curse and to swear, saying, I know not this man of whom ye speak. 72 And the second time the cock crew. And Peter called to mind the word that Jesus said unto him, Before the cock crow twice, thou shalt deny me thrice. And when he thought thereon, he wept.	59 And about the space of one hour after another confidently affirmed, saying, Of a truth this fellow also was with him: for he is a Galilaean. 60 And Peter said, Man, I know not what thou sayest. And immediately, while he yet spake, the cock crew. 61 And the Lord turned, and looked upon Peter. And Peter remembered the word of the Lord, how he had said unto him, Before the cock crow, thou shalt deny me thrice. 62 And Peter went out, and wept bitterly. 63 And the men that held Jesus mocked him, and smote him. 64 And when they had blindfolded him, they struck him on the face, and asked him, saying, Prophesy, who is it that smote thee? 65 And many other things blasphemously spake they against him.	**26** One of the servants of the high priest, being his kinsman whose ear Peter cut off, saith, Did not I see thee in the garden with him? **27** Peter then denied again: and immediately the cock crew.

Reading for Day 6

Christ Before Pilate

Matthew	Mark	Luke	John
CHAPTER 27 1 When the morning was come, all the chief priests and elders of the people took counsel against Jesus to put him to death: 2 And when they had bound him, they led him away, and delivered him to Pontius Pilate the governor.	**CHAPTER 15** 1 And straightway in the morning the chief priests held a consultation with the elders and scribes and the whole council, and bound Jesus, and carried him away, and delivered him to Pilate.	**CHAPTER 23** 1 And the whole multitude of them arose, and led him unto Pilate.	28 Then led they Jesus from Caiaphas unto the hall of judgment: and it was early; and they themselves went not into the judgment hall, lest they should be defiled; but that they might eat the passover. 29 Pilate then went out unto them, and said, What accusation bring ye against this man? 30 They answered and said unto him, If he were not a malefactor, we would not have delivered him up unto thee. 31 Then said Pilate unto them, Take ye him, and judge him according to your law. The Jews therefore said unto him, It is not lawful for us to put any man to death: 32 That the saying of Jesus might be fulfilled, which he spake, signifying what death he should die.

11 And Jesus stood before the governor: and the gover-
nor asked him, saying, Art thou the King of the Jews? And
Jesus said unto him, Thou sayest.

12 And when he was accused of the chief priests and
elders, he answered nothing.
13 Then said Pilate unto him, Hearest thou not how
many things they witness against thee?
14 And he answered him to never a word; insomuch
that the governor marvelled greatly.

3 Then Judas, which had betrayed him, when he saw
that he was condemned, repented himself, and brought
again the thirty pieces of silver to the chief priests and
elders,
4 Saying, I have sinned in that I have betrayed the inno-
cent blood. And they said, What is that to us? see thou to
that.
5 And he cast down the pieces of silver in the temple,
and departed, and went and hanged himself.
6 And the chief priests took the silver pieces, and said,
It is not lawful for to put them into the treasury, because it
is the price of blood.
7 And they took counsel, and bought with them the pot-
ter's field, to bury strangers in.
8 Wherefore that field was called, The field of blood,
unto this day.
9 Then was fulfilled that which was spoken by Jeremy
the prophet, saying, And they took the thirty pieces of sil-
ver, the price of him that was valued, whom they of the
children of Israel did value;
10 And gave them for the potter's field, as the Lord
appointed me.

2 And Pilate asked him, Art thou the King of the Jews?
And he answering said unto him, Thou sayest it.

3 And the chief priests accused him of many things: but
he answered nothing.
4 And Pilate asked him again, saying, Answerest thou
nothing? behold how many things they witness against
thee.
5 But Jesus yet answered nothing; so that Pilate mar-
velled.

2 And they began to accuse him, saying, We found this
fellow perverting the nation, and forbidding to give trib-
ute to Caesar, saying that he himself is Christ a King.

3 And Pilate asked him, saying, Art thou the King of the
Jews? And he answered him and said, Thou sayest it.

4 Then said Pilate to the chief priests and to the people,
I find no fault in this man.

5 And they were the more fierce, saying, He stirreth up
the people, teaching throughout all Jewry, beginning from
Galilee to this place.
6 When Pilate heard of Galilee, he asked whether the
man were a Galilaean.
7 And as soon as he knew that he belonged unto Herod's
jurisdiction, he sent him to Herod, who himself also was at
Jerusalem at that time.

33 Then Pilate entered into the judgment hall again,
and called Jesus, and said unto him, Art thou the King of
the Jews?
34 Jesus answered him, Sayest thou this thing of thyself,
or did others tell it thee of me?
35 Pilate answered, Am I a Jew? Thine own nation and
the chief priests have delivered thee unto me: what hast
thou done?
36 Jesus answered, My kingdom is not of this world: if my
kingdom were of this world, then would my servants fight,
that I should not be delivered to the Jews: but now is my
kingdom not from hence.
37 Pilate therefore said unto him, Art thou a king then?
Jesus answered, Thou sayest that I am a king. To this end
was I born, and for this cause came I into the world, that I
should bear witness unto the truth. Every one that is of the
truth heareth my voice.

38 Pilate saith unto him, What is truth? And when he
had said this, he went out again unto the Jews, and saith
unto them, I find in him no fault at all.

Christ Before Herod

Matthew 27	Mark 15	Luke 23	John 18
		8 And when Herod saw Jesus, he was exceeding glad: for he was desirous to see him of a long season, because he had heard many things of him; and he hoped to have seen some miracle done by him. 9 Then he questioned with him in many words; but he answered him nothing. 10 And the chief priests and scribes stood and vehemently accused him. 11 And Herod with his men of war set him at nought, and mocked him, and arrayed him in a gorgeous robe, and sent him again to Pilate. 12 And the same day Pilate and Herod were made friends together: for before they were at enmity between themselves.	

Christ Before Pilate, Second Time

Matthew 27	Mark 15	Luke 23	John 18
		13 And Pilate, when he had called together the chief priests and the rulers and the people, 14 Said unto them, Ye have brought this man unto me, as one that perverteth the people: and, behold, I, having examined him before you, have found no fault in this man touching those things whereof ye accuse him: 15 No, nor yet Herod: for I sent you to him; and, lo, nothing worthy of death is done unto him. 16 I will therefore chastise him, and release him. 17 (For of necessity he must release one unto them at the feast.)	
15 Now at that feast the governor was wont to release unto the people a prisoner, whom they would. 16 And they had then a notable prisoner, called Barabbas.	6 Now at that feast he released unto them one prisoner, whomsoever they desired. 7 And there was one named Barabbas, which lay bound with them that had made insurrection with him, who had committed murder in the insurrection. 8 And the multitude crying aloud began to desire him to do as he had ever done unto them.		
17 Therefore when they were gathered together, Pilate said unto them, Whom will ye that I release unto you? Barabbas, or Jesus which is called Christ?	9 But Pilate answered them, saying, Will ye that I release unto you the King of the Jews?		39 But ye have a custom, that I should release unto you one at the passover: will ye therefore that I release unto you the King of the Jews?
18 For he knew that for envy they had delivered him. 19 When he was set down on the judgment seat, his wife sent unto him, saying, Have thou nothing to do with that just man: for I have suffered many things this day in a dream because of him.	10 For he knew that the chief priests had delivered him for envy.		
20 But the chief priests and elders persuaded the multitude that they should ask Barabbas, and destroy Jesus.	11 But the chief priests moved the people, that he should rather release Barabbas unto them.		
21 The governor answered and said unto them, Whether of the twain will ye that I release unto you? They said, Barabbas.		18 And they cried out all at once, saying, Away with this man, and release unto us Barabbas: 19 (Who for a certain sedition made in the city, and for murder, was cast into prison.) 20 Pilate therefore, willing to release Jesus, spake again to them.	40 Then cried they all again, saying, Not this man, but Barabbas. Now Barabbas was a robber.
22 Pilate saith unto them, What shall I do then with Jesus which is called Christ? They all say unto him, Let him be crucified.	12 And Pilate answered and said again unto them, What will ye then that I shall do unto him whom ye call the King of the Jews? 13 And they cried out again, Crucify him.		
23 And the governor said, Why, what evil hath he done? But they cried out the more, saying, Let him be crucified.	14 Then Pilate said unto them, Why, what evil hath he done? And they cried out the more exceedingly, Crucify him.	21 But they cried, saying, Crucify him, crucify him. 22 And he said unto them the third time, Why, what evil hath he done? I have found no cause of death in him: I will therefore chastise him, and let him go.	

24 When Pilate saw that he could prevail nothing, but that rather a tumult was made, he took water, and washed his hands before the multitude, saying, I am innocent of the blood of this just person: see ye to it.
25 Then answered all the people, and said, His blood be on us, and on our children.
26 Then released he Barabbas unto them: and when he had scourged Jesus, he delivered him to be crucified.

15 And so Pilate, willing to content the people, released Barabbas unto them, and delivered Jesus, when he had scourged him, to be crucified.

23 And they were instant with loud voices, requiring that he might be crucified. And the voices of them and of the chief priests prevailed.

24 And Pilate gave sentence that it should be as they required.
25 And he released unto them him that for sedition and murder was cast into prison, whom they had desired; but he delivered Jesus to their will.

Christ Scourged and Mocked by Soldiers

27 Then the soldiers of the governor took Jesus into the common hall, and gathered unto him the whole band of soldiers.
28 And they stripped him, and put on him a scarlet robe.
29 And when they had platted a crown of thorns, they put it upon his head, and a reed in his right hand: and they bowed the knee before him, and mocked him, saying, Hail, King of the Jews!
30 And they spit upon him, and took the reed, and smote him on the head.

16 And the soldiers led him away into the hall, called Praetorium; and they call together the whole band.

17 And they clothed him with purple, and platted a crown of thorns, and put it about his head,
18 And began to salute him, Hail, King of the Jews!
19 And they smote him on the head with a reed, and did spit upon him, and bowing their knees worshipped him.

CHAPTER 19

1 Then Pilate therefore took Jesus, and scourged him.

2 And the soldiers platted a crown of thorns, and put it on his head, and they put on him a purple robe,
3 And said, Hail, King of the Jews! and they smote him with their hands.
4 Pilate therefore went forth again, and saith unto them, Behold, I bring him forth to you, that ye may know that I find no fault in him.
5 Then came Jesus forth, wearing the crown of thorns, and the purple robe. And Pilate saith unto them, Behold the man!
6 When the chief priests therefore and officers saw him, they cried out, saying, Crucify him, crucify him. Pilate saith unto them, Take ye him, and crucify him: for I find no fault in him.
7 The Jews answered him, We have a law, and by our law he ought to die, because he made himself the Son of God.
8 When Pilate therefore heard that saying, he was the more afraid;
9 And went again into the judgment hall, and saith unto Jesus, Whence art thou? But Jesus gave him no answer.
10 Then saith Pilate unto him, Speakest thou not unto me? knowest thou not that I have power to crucify thee, and have power to release thee?
11 Jesus answered, Thou couldest have no power at all against me, except it were given thee from above: therefore he that delivered me unto thee hath the greater sin.
12 And from thenceforth Pilate sought to release him: but the Jews cried out, saying, If thou let this man go, thou art not Caesar's friend: whosoever maketh himself a king speaketh against Caesar.
13 When Pilate therefore heard that saying, he brought Jesus forth, and sat down in the judgment seat in a place that is called the Pavement, but in the Hebrew, Gabbatha.
14 And it was the preparation of the passover, and about the sixth hour: and he saith unto the Jews, Behold your King!
15 But they cried out, Away with him, away with him, crucify him. Pilate saith unto them, Shall I crucify your King? The chief priests answered, We have no king but Caesar.

Walk to Golgotha

Matthew 27	Mark 15	Luke 23	John 19
31 And after that they had mocked him, they took the robe off from him, and put his own raiment on him, and led him away to crucify him. 32 And as they came out, they found a man of Cyrene, Simon by name: him they compelled to bear his cross.	20 And when they had mocked him, they took off the purple from him, and put his own clothes on him, and led him out to crucify him. 21 And they compel one Simon a Cyrenian, who passed by, coming out of the country, the father of Alexander and Rufus, to bear his cross.	26 And as they led him away, they laid hold upon one Simon, a Cyrenian, coming out of the country, and on him they laid the cross, that he might bear it after Jesus.	16 Then delivered he him therefore unto them to be crucified. And they took Jesus, and led him away.
		27 And there followed him a great company of people, and of women, which also bewailed and lamented him. 28 But Jesus turning unto them said, Daughters of Jerusalem, weep not for me, but weep for yourselves, and for your children. 29 For, behold, the days are coming, in the which they shall say, Blessed are the barren, and the wombs that never bare, and the paps which never gave suck. 30 Then shall they begin to say to the mountains, Fall on us; and to the hills, Cover us. 31 For if they do these things in a green tree, what shall be done in the dry? 32 And there were also two other, malefactors, led with him to be put to death.	

Crucifixion

Matthew 27	Mark 15	Luke 23	John 19
33 And when they were come unto a place called Golgotha, that is to say, a place of a skull, **38** Then were there two thieves crucified with him, one on the right hand, and another on the left.	22 And they bring him unto the place Golgotha, which is, being interpreted, The place of a skull. **27** And with him they crucify two thieves; the one on his right hand, and the other on his left. **28** And the scripture was fulfilled, which saith, And he was numbered with the transgressors.	33 And when they were come to the place, which is called Calvary, there they crucified him, and the malefactors, one on the right hand, and the other on the left.	17 And he bearing his cross went forth into a place called the place of a skull, which is called in the Hebrew Golgotha: 18 Where they crucified him, and two other with him, on either side one, and Jesus in the midst.
37 And set up over his head his accusation written, This Is Jesus the KIng of the Jews.	**26** And the superscription of his accusation was written over, The King of the Jews.	**38** And a superscription also was written over him in letters of Greek, and Latin, and Hebrew, This Is the King of the Jews.	19 And Pilate wrote a title, and put it on the cross. And the writing was, Jesus of Nazareth the King of the Jews. 20 This title then read many of the Jews: for the place where Jesus was crucified was nigh to the city: and it was written in Hebrew, and Greek, and Latin. 21 Then said the chief priests of the Jews to Pilate, Write not, The King of the Jews; but that he said, I am King of the Jews. 22 Pilate answered, What I have written I have written.
34 They gave him vinegar to drink mingled with gall: and when he had tasted thereof, he would not drink.	23 And they gave him to drink wine mingled with myrrh: but he received it not.	**36** And the soldiers also mocked him, coming to him, and offering him vinegar, **37** And saying, If thou be the king of the Jews, save thyself.	
35 And they crucified him, and parted his garments, casting lots: that it might be fulfilled which was spoken by the prophet, They parted my garments among them, and upon my vesture did they cast lots. 36 And sitting down they watched him there;	24 And when they had crucified him, they parted his garments, casting lots upon them, what every man should take.	34 Then said Jesus, Father, forgive them; for they know not what they do. And they parted his raiment, and cast lots.	23 Then the soldiers, when they had crucified Jesus, took his garments, and made four parts, to every soldier a part; and also his coat: now the coat was without seam, woven from the top throughout. 24 They said therefore among themselves, Let us not rend it, but cast lots for it, whose it shall be: that the scripture might be fulfilled, which saith, They parted my raiment among them, and for my vesture they did cast lots. These things therefore the soldiers did.
39 And they that passed by reviled him, wagging their heads, 40 And saying, Thou that destroyest the temple, and buildest it in three days, save thyself. If thou be the Son of God, come down from the cross.	25 And it was the third hour, and they crucified him. 29 And they that passed by railed on him, wagging their heads, and saying, Ah, thou that destroyest the temple, and buildest it in three days,	35 And the people stood beholding. And the rulers also with them derided him, saying, He saved others; let him save himself, if he be Christ, the chosen of God.	

41 Likewise also the chief priests mocking him, with the scribes and elders, said,

42 He saved others; himself he cannot save. If he be the King of Israel, let him now come down from the cross, and we will believe him.

43 He trusted in God; let him deliver him now, if he will have him: for he said, I am the Son of God.

44 The thieves also, which were crucified with him, cast the same in his teeth.

45 Now from the sixth hour there was darkness over all the land unto the ninth hour.

46 And about the ninth hour Jesus cried with a loud voice, saying, Eli, Eli, lama sabachthani? that is to say, My God, my God, why hast thou forsaken me?

47 Some of them that stood there, when they heard that, said, This man calleth for Elias.

48 And straightway one of them ran, and took a spunge, and filled it with vinegar, and put it on a reed, and gave him to drink.

49 The rest said, Let be, let us see whether Elias will come to save him.

50 Jesus, when he had cried again with a loud voice, yielded up the ghost.

51 And, behold, the veil of the temple was rent in twain from the top to the bottom; and the earth did quake, and the rocks rent;

52 And the graves were opened; and many bodies of the saints which slept arose,

53 And came out of the graves after his resurrection, and went into the holy city, and appeared unto many.

54 Now when the centurion, and they that were with him, watching Jesus, saw the earthquake, and those things that were done, they feared greatly, saying, Truly this was the Son of God.

30 Save thyself, and come down from the cross.

31 Likewise also the chief priests mocking said among themselves with the scribes, He saved others; himself he cannot save.

32 Let Christ the King of Israel descend now from the cross, that we may see and believe. And they that were crucified with him reviled him.

33 And when the sixth hour was come, there was darkness over the whole land until the ninth hour.

34 And at the ninth hour Jesus cried with a loud voice, saying, Eloi, Eloi, lama sabachthani? which is, being interpreted, My God, my God, why hast thou forsaken me?

35 And some of them that stood by, when they heard it, said, Behold, he calleth Elias.

36 And one ran and filled a spunge full of vinegar, and put it on a reed, and gave him to drink, saying, Let alone; let us see whether Elias will come to take him down.

37 And Jesus cried with a loud voice, and gave up the ghost.

38 And the veil of the temple was rent in twain from the top to the bottom.

39 And when the centurion, which stood over against him, saw that he so cried out, and gave up the ghost, he said, Truly this man was the Son of God.

39 And one of the malefactors which were hanged railed on him, saying, If thou be Christ, save thyself and us.

40 But the other answering rebuked him, saying, Dost not thou fear God, seeing thou art in the same condemnation?

41 And we indeed justly; for we receive the due reward of our deeds: but this man hath done nothing amiss.

42 And he said unto Jesus, Lord, remember me when thou comest into thy kingdom.

43 And Jesus said unto him, Verily I say unto thee, To day shalt thou be with me in paradise.

44 And it was about the sixth hour, and there was a darkness over all the earth until the ninth hour.

45 And the sun was darkened, and the veil of the temple was rent in the midst.

46 And when Jesus had cried with a loud voice, he said, Father, into thy hands I commend my spirit: and having said thus, he gave up the ghost.

47 Now when the centurion saw what was done, he glorified God, saying, Certainly this was a righteous man.

25 Now there stood by the cross of Jesus his mother, and his mother's sister, Mary the wife of Cleophas, and Mary Magdalene.

26 When Jesus therefore saw his mother, and the disciple standing by, whom he loved, he saith unto his mother, Woman, behold thy son!

27 Then saith he to the disciple, Behold thy mother! And from that hour that disciple took her unto his own home.

28 After this, Jesus knowing that all things were now accomplished, that the scripture might be fulfilled, saith, I thirst.

29 Now there was set a vessel full of vinegar: and they filled a spunge with vinegar, and put it upon hyssop, and put it to his mouth.

30 When Jesus therefore had received the vinegar, he said, It is finished: and he bowed his head, and gave up the ghost.

BURIAL

Matthew 27	Mark 15	Luke 23	John 19
			31 The Jews therefore, because it was the preparation, that the bodies should not remain upon the cross on the sabbath day, (for that sabbath day was an high day,) besought Pilate that their legs might be broken, and that they might be taken away. 32 Then came the soldiers, and brake the legs of the first, and of the other which was crucified with him. 33 But when they came to Jesus, and saw that he was dead already, they brake not his legs: 34 But one of the soldiers with a spear pierced his side, and forthwith came there out blood and water. 35 And he that saw it bare record, and his record is true: and he knoweth that he saith true, that ye might believe. 36 For these things were done, that the scripture should be fulfilled, A bone of him shall not be broken. 37 And again another scripture saith, They shall look on him whom they pierced.
55 And many women were there beholding afar off, which followed Jesus from Galilee, ministering unto him: 56 Among which was Mary Magdalene, and Mary the mother of James and Joses, and the mother of Zebedee's children.	40 There were also women looking on afar off: among whom was Mary Magdalene, and Mary the mother of James the less and of Joses, and Salome; 41 (Who also, when he was in Galilee, followed him, and ministered unto him;) and many other women which came up with him unto Jerusalem.	48 And all the people that came together to that sight, beholding the things which were done, smote their breasts, and returned. 49 And all his acquaintance, and the women that followed him from Galilee, stood afar off, beholding these things.	
57 When the even was come, there came a rich man of Arimathaea, named Joseph, who also himself was Jesus' disciple: 58 He went to Pilate, and begged the body of Jesus. Then Pilate commanded the body to be delivered.	42 And now when the even was come, because it was the preparation, that is, the day before the sabbath, 43 Joseph of Arimathaea, an honourable counsellor, which also waited for the kingdom of God, came, and went in boldly unto Pilate, and craved the body of Jesus.	50 And, behold, there was a man named Joseph, a counsellor; and he was a good man, and a just: 51 (The same had not consented to the counsel and deed of them;) he was of Arimathaea, a city of the Jews: who also himself waited for the kingdom of God. 52 This man went unto Pilate, and begged the body of Jesus.	38 And after this Joseph of Arimathaea, being a disciple of Jesus, but secretly for fear of the Jews, besought Pilate that he might take away the body of Jesus: and Pilate gave him leave. He came therefore, and took the body of Jesus.
	44 And Pilate marvelled if he were already dead: and calling unto him the centurion, he asked him whether he had been any while dead. 45 And when he knew it of the centurion, he gave the body to Joseph.		
59 And when Joseph had taken the body, he wrapped it in a clean linen cloth,	46 And he bought fine linen, and took him down, and wrapped him in the linen, and laid him in a sepulchre which was hewn out of a rock, and rolled a stone unto the door of the sepulchre.	53 And he took it down, and wrapped it in linen, and laid it in a sepulchre that was hewn in stone, wherein never man before was laid. 54 And that day was the preparation, and the sabbath drew on.	39 And there came also Nicodemus, which at the first came to Jesus by night, and brought a mixture of myrrh and aloes, about an hundred pound weight. 40 Then took they the body of Jesus, and wound it in linen clothes with the spices, as the manner of the Jews is to bury. 41 Now in the place where he was crucified there was a garden; and in the garden a new sepulchre, wherein was never man yet laid. 42 There laid they Jesus therefore because of the Jews' preparation day; for the sepulchre was nigh at hand.
60 And laid it in his own new tomb, which he had hewn out in the rock: and he rolled a great stone to the door of the sepulchre, and departed. 61 And there was Mary Magdalene, and the other Mary, sitting over against the sepulchre.	47 And Mary Magdalene and Mary the mother of Joses beheld where he was laid.	55 And the women also, which came with him from Galilee, followed after, and beheld the sepulchre, and how his body was laid. 56 And they returned, and prepared spices and ointments; and rested the sabbath day according to the commandment.	

Reading for Day 7

62 Now the next day, that followed the day of the preparation, the chief priests and Pharisees came together unto Pilate,
63 Saying, Sir, we remember that that deceiver said, while he was yet alive, After three days I will rise again.
64 Command therefore that the sepulchre be made sure until the third day, lest his disciples come by night, and steal him away, and say unto the people, He is risen from the dead: so the last error shall be worse than the first.
65 Pilate said unto them, Ye have a watch: go your way, make it as sure as ye can.
66 So they went, and made the sepulchre sure, sealing the stone, and setting a watch.

Reading for Day 8

CHAPTER 28

1 In the end of the sabbath, as it began to dawn toward the first day of the week, came Mary Magdalene and the other Mary to see the sepulchre.
2 And, behold, there was a great earthquake: for the angel of the Lord descended from heaven, and came and rolled back the stone from the door, and sat upon it.

CHAPTER 24

1 Now upon the first day of the week, very early in the morning, they came unto the sepulchre, bringing the spices which they had prepared, and certain others with them.
2 And they found the stone rolled away from the sepulchre.

12 Then arose Peter, and ran unto the sepulchre; and stooping down, he beheld the linen clothes laid by themselves, and departed, wondering in himself at that which was come to pass.
24 And certain of them which were with us went to the sepulchre, and found it even so as the women had said: but him they saw not.

CHAPTER 20

1 The first day of the week cometh Mary Magdalene early, when it was yet dark, unto the sepulchre, and seeth the stone taken away from the sepulchre.
2 Then she runneth, and cometh to Simon Peter, and to the other disciple, whom Jesus loved, and saith unto them, They have taken away the Lord out of the sepulchre, and we know not where they have laid him.
3 Peter therefore went forth, and that other disciple, and came to the sepulchre.
4 So they ran both together: and the other disciple did outrun Peter, and came first to the sepulchre.
5 And he stooping down, and looking in, saw the linen clothes lying; yet went he not in.
6 Then cometh Simon Peter following him, and went into the sepulchre, and seeth the linen clothes lie,
7 And the napkin, that was about his head, not lying with the linen clothes, but wrapped together in a place by itself.
8 Then went in also that other disciple, which came first to the sepulchre, and he saw, and believed.
9 For as yet they knew not the scripture, that he must rise again from the dead.
10 Then the disciples went away again unto their own home.

Appearance to Mary Magdalene

11 But Mary stood without at the sepulchre weeping: and as she wept, she stooped down, and looked into the sepulchre,
12 And seeth two angels in white sitting, the one at the head, and the other at the feet, where the body of Jesus had lain.

Matthew 28

1 In the end of the sabbath, as it began to dawn toward the first day of the week, came Mary Magdalene and the other Mary to see the sepulchre.

2 And, behold, there was a great earthquake: for the angel of the Lord descended from heaven, and came and rolled back the stone from the door, and sat upon it.
3 His countenance was like lightning, and his raiment white as snow:
4 And for fear of him the keepers did shake, and became as dead men.

5 And the angel answered and said unto the women, Fear not ye: for I know that ye seek Jesus, which was crucified.
6 He is not here: for he is risen, as he said. Come, see the place where the Lord lay.

7 And go quickly, and tell his disciples that he is risen from the dead; and, behold, he goeth before you into Galilee; there shall ye see him: lo, I have told you.

Mark 16

CHAPTER 16

10 And she went and told them that had been with him, as they mourned and wept.
11 And they, when they had heard that he was alive, and had been seen of her, believed not.
1 And when the sabbath was past, Mary Magdalene, and Mary the mother of James, and Salome, had bought sweet spices, that they might come and anoint him.
2 And very early in the morning the first day of the week, they came unto the sepulchre at the rising of the sun.
3 And they said among themselves, Who shall roll us away the stone from the door of the sepulchre?

4 And when they looked, they saw that the stone was rolled away: for it was very great.

5 And entering into the sepulchre, they saw a young man sitting on the right side, clothed in a long white garment; and they were affrighted.
6 And he saith unto them, Be not affrighted: Ye seek Jesus of Nazareth, which was crucified: he is risen; he is not here: behold the place where they laid him.

7 But go your way, tell his disciples and Peter that he goeth before you into Galilee: there shall ye see him, as he said unto you.
8 And they went out quickly, and fled from the sepulchre; for they trembled and were amazed: neither said they any thing to any man; for they were afraid.

Luke 24

3 And they entered in, and found not the body of the Lord Jesus.
4 And it came to pass, as they were much perplexed thereabout, behold, two men stood by them in shining garments:
5 And as they were afraid, and bowed down their faces to the earth, they said unto them, Why seek ye the living among the dead?
6 He is not here, but is risen: remember how he spake unto you when he was yet in Galilee,
7 Saying, The Son of man must be delivered into the hands of sinful men, and be crucified, and the third day rise again.
8 And they remembered his words,

John 20

13 And they say unto her, Woman, why weepest thou? She saith unto them, Because they have taken away my Lord, and I know not where they have laid him.
14 And when she had thus said, she turned herself back, and saw Jesus standing, and knew not that it was Jesus.
15 Jesus saith unto her, Woman, why weepest thou? whom seekest thou? She, supposing him to be the gardener, saith unto him, Sir, if thou have borne him hence, tell me where thou hast laid him, and I will take him away.
16 Jesus saith unto her, Mary. She turned herself, and saith unto him, Rabboni; which is to say, Master.
17 Jesus saith unto her, Touch me not; for I am not yet ascended to my Father: but go to my brethren, and say unto them, I ascend unto my Father, and your Father; and to my God, and your God.
18 Mary Magdalene came and told the disciples that she had seen the Lord, and that he had spoken these things unto her.

8 And they departed quickly from the sepulchre with
fear and great joy; and did run to bring his disciples word.
9 And as they went to tell his disciples, behold, Jesus met
them, saying, All hail. And they came and held him by the
feet, and worshipped him.
10 Then said Jesus unto them, Be not afraid: go tell my
brethren that they go into Galilee, and there shall they see
me.
11 Now when they were going, behold, some of the
watch came into the city, and shewed unto the chief priests
all the things that were done.
12 And when they were assembled with the elders, and
had taken counsel, they gave large money unto the sol-
diers,
13 Saying, Say ye, His disciples came by night, and stole
him away while we slept.
14 And if this come to the governor's ears, we will per-
suade him, and secure you.
15 So they took the money, and did as they were taught:
and this saying is commonly reported among the Jews until
this day.

9 Now when Jesus was risen early the first day of the
week, he appeared first to Mary Magdalene, out of whom
he had cast seven devils.

9 And returned from the sepulchre, and told all these
things unto the eleven, and to all the rest.
10 It was Mary Magdalene, and Joanna, and Mary the
mother of James, and other women that were with them,
which told these things unto the apostles.
11 And their words seemed to them as idle tales, and
they believed them not.

Appearance on Road to Emmaus

12 After that he appeared in another form unto two of
them, as they walked, and went into the country.

13 And, behold, two of them went that same day to a
village called Emmaus, which was from Jerusalem about
threescore furlongs.
14 And they talked together of all these things which
had happened.
15 And it came to pass, that, while they communed
together and reasoned, Jesus himself drew near, and went
with them.
16 But their eyes were holden that they should not know
him.
17 And he said unto them, What manner of communi-
cations are these that ye have one to another, as ye walk,
and are sad?
18 And the one of them, whose name was Cleopas,
answering said unto him, Art thou only a stranger in
Jerusalem, and hast not known the things which are come
to pass there in these days?
19 And he said unto them, What things? And they said
unto him, Concerning Jesus of Nazareth, which was a
prophet mighty in deed and word before God and all the
people:
20 And how the chief priests and our rulers delivered
him to be condemned to death, and have crucified him.
21 But we trusted that it had been he which should have
redeemed Israel: and beside all this, to day is the third day
since these things were done.
22 Yea, and certain women also of our company made us
astonished, which were early at the sepulchre;
23 And when they found not his body, they came, say-

Mark 16

13 And they went and told it unto the residue: neither believed they them.

Luke 24

ing, that they had also seen a vision of angels, which said that he was alive.
24 And certain of them which were with us went to the sepulchre, and found it even so as the women had said: but him they saw not.
25 Then he said unto them, O fools, and slow of heart to believe all that the prophets have spoken:
26 Ought not Christ to have suffered these things, and to enter into his glory?
27 And beginning at Moses and all the prophets, he expounded unto them in all the scriptures the things concerning himself.
28 And they drew nigh unto the village, whither they went: and he made as though he would have gone further.
29 But they constrained him, saying, Abide with us: for it is toward evening, and the day is far spent. And he went in to tarry with them.
30 And it came to pass, as he sat at meat with them, he took bread, and blessed it, and brake, and gave to them.
31 And their eyes were opened, and they knew him; and he vanished out of their sight.
32 And they said one to another, Did not our heart burn within us, while he talked with us by the way, and while he opened to us the scriptures?
33 And they rose up the same hour, and returned to Jerusalem, and found the eleven gathered together, and them that were with them,
34 Saying, The Lord is risen indeed, and hath appeared to Simon.
35 And they told what things were done in the way, and how he was known of them in breaking of bread.

Appearance to Eleven in Jerusalem

Mark 16

14 Afterward he appeared unto the eleven as they sat at meat, and upbraided them with their unbelief and hardness of heart, because they believed not them which had seen him after he was risen.

Luke 24

36 And as they thus spake, Jesus himself stood in the midst of them, and saith unto them, Peace be unto you.

37 But they were terrified and affrighted, and supposed that they had seen a spirit.
38 And he said unto them, Why are ye troubled? and why do thoughts arise in your hearts?
39 Behold my hands and my feet, that it is I myself: handle me, and see; for a spirit hath not flesh and bones, as ye see me have.
40 And when he had thus spoken, he shewed them his hands and his feet.

41 And while they yet believed not for joy, and wondered, he said unto them, Have ye here any meat?
42 And they gave him a piece of a broiled fish, and of an honeycomb.
43 And he took it, and did eat before them.

John 20

19 Then the same day at evening, being the first day of the week, when the doors were shut where the disciples were assembled for fear of the Jews, came Jesus and stood in the midst, and saith unto them, Peace be unto you.

20 And when he had so said, he shewed unto them his hands and his side. Then were the disciples glad, when they saw the Lord.

44 And he said unto them, These are the words which I
spake unto you, while I was yet with you, that all things
must be fulfilled, which were written in the law of Moses,
and in the prophets, and in the psalms, concerning me.
45 Then opened he their understanding, that they might
understand the scriptures,
46 And said unto them, Thus it is written, and thus it
behoved Christ to suffer, and to rise from the dead the
third day:
47 And that repentance and remission of sins should be
preached in his name among all nations, beginning at
Jerusalem.
48 And ye are witnesses of these things.
49 And, behold, I send the promise of my Father upon
you: but tarry ye in the city of Jerusalem, until ye be
endued with power from on high.

21 Then said Jesus to them again, Peace be unto you: as
my Father hath sent me, even so send I you.
22 And when he had said this, he breathed on them, and
saith unto them, Receive ye the Holy Ghost:
23 Whose soever sins ye remit, they are remitted unto
them; and whose soever sins ye retain, they are retained.

Useful Reference Materials for Children, Youth, and Adults

Helps for Children and Their Parents

Books

Note: Some of these books reflect a perspective different from that taught in The Church of Jesus Christ of Latter-day Saints (i.e. concept of the trinity vs. three distinct members of the Godhead). Depending on the age of the child enjoying the book with me, I have either changed the text slightly as I have read it to reflect what we believe is true, or I have read it as written and then discussed the differing beliefs with him or her.

Embry, Margaret. *Everyday Life in Bible Times: Work, Worship, and War.* Nashville: T. Nelson, 1994.

———. *Growing Up in Bible Times: Families at Work and at Play.* Nashville: T. Nelson, 1995.

Fosdick, Harry Emerson. *Jesus of Nazareth.* New York: Random House, 1959.

Hurlbut, Jesse Lyman. *Hurlbut's Story of the Bible for Young and Old: A Continuous Narrative of the Scriptures Told in One Hundred Eighty-six Stories.* (Revised edition) Grand Rapids, Mich.: Zondervan Publishing House, 1974.

L'engle, Madeleine. *The Glorious Impossible.* New York: Simon and Schuster, 1990.

McConkie, Joseph Fielding. *Gospel Symbolism.* Salt Lake City: Bookcraft, 1985.

Millet, Robert L. *Parables and Other Teaching Stories.* Salt Lake City: Shadow Mountain, 1999.

New Testament Stories. Salt Lake City: The Church of Jesus Christ of Latter-day Saints, 1980.

Scripture Stories. Salt Lake City: The Church of Jesus Christ of Latter-day Saints, 1980.

Sheldon, Charles M. *In His Steps.* Harold J. Chadwick, editor. North Brunswick, N.J.: Bridge-Logos Publishers, 2000. (First published in the 1800s, this book is available today from a number of publishers. Although this book is fiction, the premise is compelling and the conclusions drawn generate a lot of discussion.)

Articles

Holland, Jeffery R. "Friend to Friend: The Cactus, the Cross, and Easter." *Friend,* April 1980, 6–7.

Schugk, Marita. "Easter Story." *Friend,* April 1992, 8–10.

Wardell, Julie. "The First Easter." *Friend,* April 1988, 20–21.

Audiotapes

Perry, Janice Kapp; Perry, Steven Kapp; Payne Marvin. *Scripture Scouts: New Testament, Tapes 1–3.* "Musical Adventures in the New Testament." Salt Lake City: Deseret Book Company, 1992.

Videotapes

"Animal Sacrifice and the Atonement." *Old Testament Video Presentations.* (Lesson 13.) Church Distribution #53224. (This video clip teaches the relationship between animal sacrifice and Christ's atonement in the context of a fictional teenager's life.)

Easter Dream. Church Distribution #53067. (This video is a short fictional story about a boy who learns to cope with his father's death through a dream he has about the Atonement and Crucifixion.)

The Lamb of God. Church Distribution #53586.

"The Mediator." *Book of Mormon Video Presentations.* (Lesson 28.) Church Distribution #53911. (This video clip portrays an analogy of the Atonement used by President Boyd K. Packer.)

New Testament Video Presentations. Church Distribution #53914.

Helps for Personal and Background Study

Books

Brown, Lewis. *The Graphic Bible.* New York: The Macmillan Company, 1951.

Callister, Tad R. *The Infinite Atonement.* Salt Lake City: Deseret Book, 2000.

The Life and Teachings of Jesus and His Apostles. Course manual, Religion 211–212. Salt Lake City: The Church of Jesus Christ of Latter-day Saints, 1979.

Robinson, Stephen E. *Believing Christ.* Salt Lake City: Deseret Book, 1992.

Smith, William. *A Dictionary of the Bible.* Rev. and ed. F. N. and M. A. Peloubet. Nashville: Nelson Publishers, 1979.

Talmage, James. *Jesus the Christ.* (Classics in Mormon Literature) Salt Lake City: Deseret Book, 1982.

Telushkin, Joseph. *Jewish Literacy: The Most Important Things to Know about the Jewish Religion, Its People, and Its History.* New York: William Morrow and Company, 1991.

Articles

Hafen, Bruce. "Beauty for Ashes." *Ensign,* April 1990, 7–13.

Hunter, Howard W. "Christ, Our Passover." *Ensign,* May 1985, 17–18.

Patch, Robert C. "I Have a Question." *Ensign,* April 1982, 29–31.

Peterson, Mark E. "Creator and Savior." *Ensign,* May 1983, 63–65.

Pratt, John P. "The Restoration of Priesthood Keys on Easter 1836, Part 1: Dating the First Easter." *Ensign,* June 1985, 59–68.

———. "The Restoration of Priesthood Keys on Easter 1836, Part 2: Symbolism of Passover and of Elijah's Return." *Ensign,* July 1985, 55–64.

Treseder, Terry W. "Passover Promises Fulfilled in the Last Supper." *Ensign,* April 1990, 19–23.

Warner, Dorothy D. "Exploring: Palms for the Lord," *Friend,* March 1996, 26–27.

The City of Jerusalem in Jesus' Day

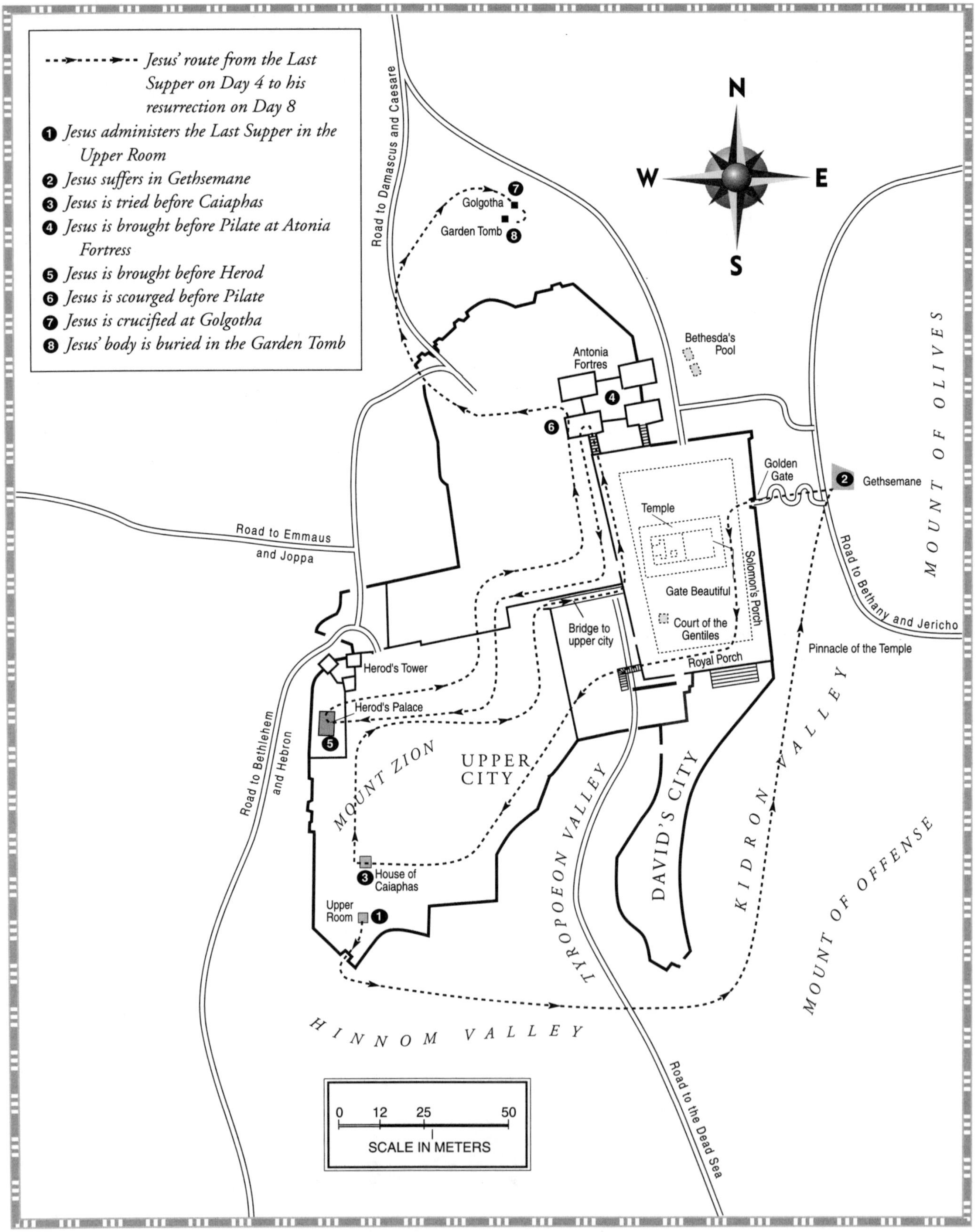

Maps courtesy of Tom Child. Used with permission.

The Holy Land at the Time of Jesus

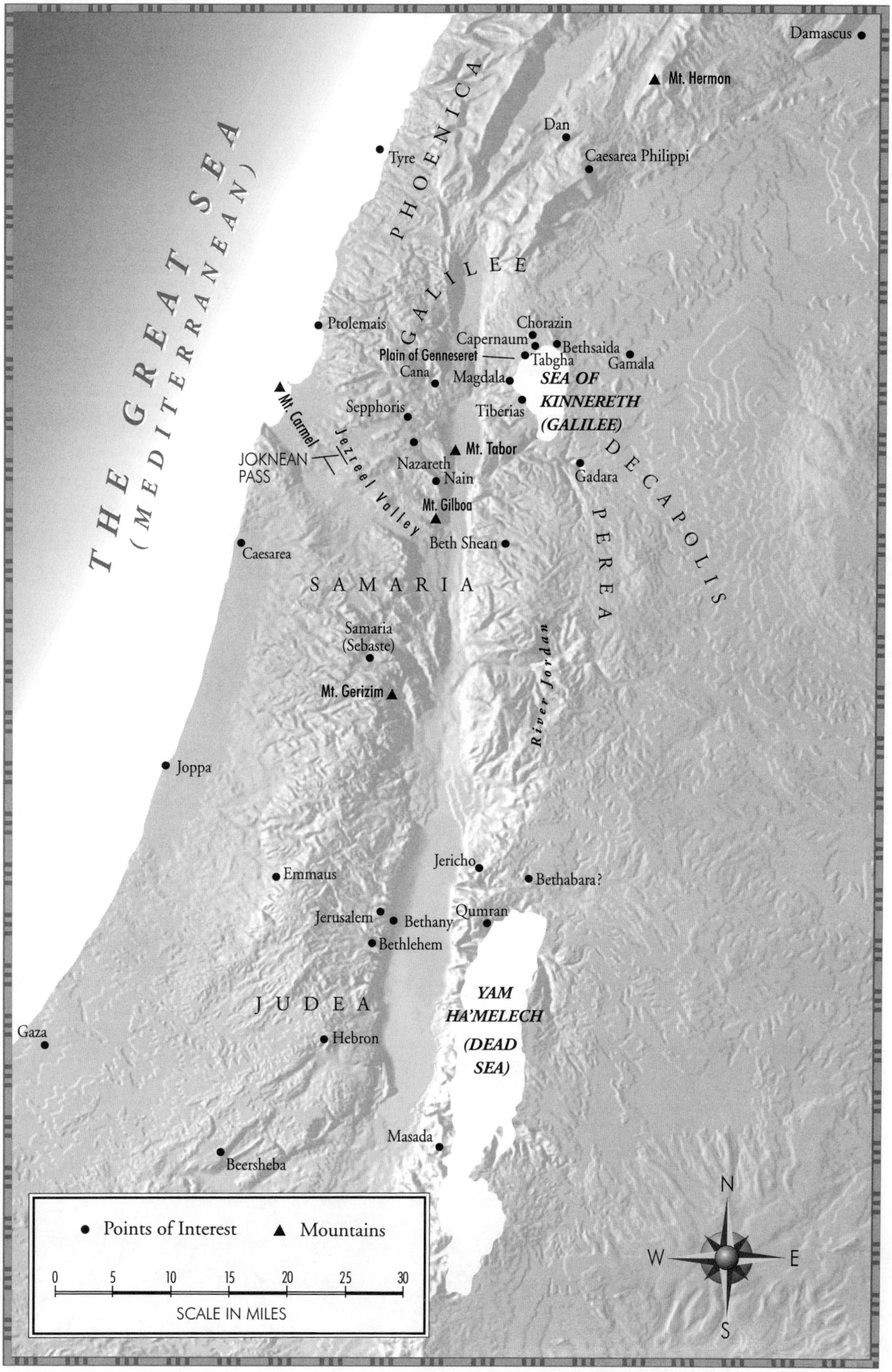